A Good
<u>Walk Spoiled</u>

To Amber, Rory, Lara and Ross

A Good Walk Spoiled

A Book of Golf Quotes

Myles Dungan

POOLBEG

Published in 1994 by
Poolbeg Press Ltd,
Knocksedan House,
123 Baldoyle Industrial Estate,
Dublin 13, Ireland

A catalogue record for this book is available from the British Library.

ISBN 1 85371 427 5

Cover photography by Gillian Buckley,
Poolbeg Group Services Ltd & Repro Link
Cover design by Poolbeg Group Services Ltd
Set by Poolbeg Group Services Ltd in Garamond 9.5/13
Printed by Colour Books Ltd, Baldoyle Industrial Estate, Baldoyle, Dublin 13.

CONTENTS

Foreword

I don't suppose it has occurred to you to make the enquiry – and, when all is said and done, why should it? But if by chance you were to ask me for my definition of a mixed blessing my reply would be: a visit to Ireland. I have been inordinately fortunate in that my work is my pleasure, and vice versa, and both require me to make frequent trips to Ireland, a place for which I seem to have a spiritual affinity. As the plane banks over the Howth peninsula and I look down and identify the links of Royal Dublin, Portmarnock, St Annes and Sutton I experience a *frisson* of excited anticipation. What magic or mischief or mayhem shall I encounter this time? Ireland is always an adventure for me and I have had some memorable adventures, notably the occasion during my portly period when I concealed my spreading girth within the ample folds of a flasher mac and a drunk mistook me for the Reverend Ian Paisley in McDonnell's bar in Cork. In the context of mixed blessings that incident could have gone either way, downside or upside, and in the end it turned out well enough. The absolute certainty of a downside happens soon after the plane lands. Somebody, it might be a customs man, or a porter, or a taxi driver, says something which hits me with the force of a shillelagh. It may be an arresting turn of phrase, or a shaft of vivid verbal imagery, or an intriguing twist in the construction of a sentence. Here am I, an experienced wordsmith for whom the English language is my stock-in-trade, who has to sweat and strain for hours to write a passable piece of prose. Can you imagine how humiliating it feels to find myself in a community where everyone, man, woman or child, speaks naturally and volubly in English which sparkles with originality, wit and colour? And to think that strictly speaking English is their second language! Galling as this may be for me, it is immensely challenging for the editor who sets out to compile a book of quotations for the Irish market. Ireland must be the world's toughest market in which to make an impact with an anthology of word play. The prosaic, the banal and the humdrum would not stand a chance. There is nothing else for it; this simply has to be a good book. I wish it every success.

Peter Dobereiner

Introduction

The American writer George Plimpton has a theory about how certain sports have been well served by talented writers and an extraordinary corpus of literature. He sees the quality of writing as being in inverse proportion to the size of the ball used in the particular sport. The smaller the ball the better the writers attracted by the game. Hence the sport of baseball (ball fitting neatly into palm of hand) has inspired writers like Ring Lardner, Bernard Malamud and Philip Roth, people who should be motivated by the higher arts, not by a spit and dust game played by blue-collar Americans. Soccer on the other hand (ball not capable of being held in one hand except by people like Pat Jennings or Packie Bonner) can only claim fiction writers of the calibre of Terry Venables. (All right, so Camus was an amateur international goalkeeper, but that doesn't diminish the theory any more than does the fact that squash, about which nobody writes at all, is played with a very small ball indeed.)

All of which is by way of prologue to the assertion that golf has been well served by the journalists who write about it and the artists who fictionalise it. In addition the people who play the game (at all levels) are often urbane, cultured, articulate and witty. (Though they can also be tedious, irascible, opinionated, dogmatic, intolerant, elitist and bigoted.) Perhaps it's because golf is a game which rewards thinkers, even philosophers, that every year it produces a new crop of pithy, resigned, jocular and downright insulting quotes to add to the Golfing Collection.

Obviously this volume will mean more to the enthusiast of the game, and especially to the knowledgeable enthusiast. But, as golf has often been compared to life itself, I hope that the eternal verities contained in these 250 or so pages, will inform, entertain and amuse non-golfers (or even anti-golfers). However, because of the nature of the volume, I have not gone into great detail in the explanation of the genesis of certain quotes which might require a short essay to explain their significance. Where golfing controversies have erupted thousands of words have been written and spoken about them. I have culled what I believe to be the most interesting contributions and set them down. Those who follow the game will know what these particular quotes are about. But I would hope that the manner in which they are set out would give the non-golfer some insight into the issues involved.

Many of the sayings in these pages are like old friends. I have had them quoted to me on fairways all over Ireland. Some phrases, through frequent usage, have been wrongly ascribed to the point where they have become almost apocryphal. For example, the story of the amateur golfer who asks the well-known professional "How can I get backspin off a 3-iron?" to which the Great Man replies "How far can you hit a 3-iron?" "About 150 yards," comes the embarrassed reply. The Illustrious One responds, "Then why do you want to get backspin off it?" I have had the Fabled Pro identified to me as Sam Snead, Ben Hogan, Arnold Palmer and even Nick Faldo (among others). The incident might actually have taken place, but because so many people ascribe the punch-line to a different player it might as well be apocryphal.

All of which is by way of saying that I have done my best to put the right words into the right mouths, though there will doubtless be umpteen people who will have heard those exact words ascribed to an entirely different person. If so, don't shoot the piano player!

I am Irish and immensely proud of the contribution this tiny country of ours has made to a wonderful international game. Wherever you go in the world names like Carr, O'Connor (x 2), Bruen, Bradshaw, Darcy and latterly Clarke, Feherty, Rafferty and McGinley are instantly recognisable to true golf fans. It's a bit like golfing Esperanto, not exactly a common language but a common iconography. Add to that list the names Ballybunion, Killarney, Portmarnock, Royal Dublin, Tralee, Waterville and latterly Mount Juliet and the K Club and you need never be stuck for conversation in Anchorage, Alaska or Hokkaido, Japan.

Because these quotes have been collected, largely for the enjoyment of an Irish audience, the Irish "content" is higher than for the many similar books which have come on the market in the past. However, a desire to include references to every Irish professional or amateur international player and every Irish golf course has had to be tempered with the awareness of my brief. This is a book of quotes, not a "Who's Who". If your favourite player or your local course has not been included then it is not because he/she is not an exceptional virtuoso or it is not a wonderful track but because no especially interesting quote on that particular subject was uncovered by this editor. I have excluded the sort of "travelogue" references to just about every club in the country which describe them all as "enchanting, a wonderful challenge, a must for every true golfer" because while readers might smile or nod sagely when such a reference is made to their favourite/local course, they would be more likely to dance up and down on the book's pages as they ploughed through the 250 other, similar, references.

My thanks are due to a number of people. Kate Cruise O'Brien of Poolbeg Press for her interest in the idea behind the book, in spite of her complete non-interest in golf. To the golf/sports writers and broadcasters who chose the eighteen Irish golf holes which adorn the opening of each chapter. They were, in alphabetical order: Greg Allen, Fred Cogley, Ronan Collins, Ian Corr, John Cunningham, Tom Cryan, Dermot Gilleece, David Jones, Malachy Logan, Charlie Mulqueen, Pat O'Donovan, Peter O'Neill, Maurice Quinn, Philip Quinn, Philip Reid, Pat Ruddy, Seamus Smith and Peter Townsend. To my colleague in RTE, Aidan Butler, for access to his impressive magazine and cuttings collection and to the Head of Sport in RTE, Tim O'Connor, for allowing me to present his golf programmes in my own imperfect way.

Finally the brief essay which precedes each chapter (or hole!) is not meant, in any way, to explain what follows but simply relates to some minor aspect of the chapter content. They are my own self-indulgent flights of fancy. If you find them irritating or unhelpful simply ignore them and proceed straight to the truths and witticisms of the men and women who have far more to say about the game of golf than I have.

The Eighteen Best Holes

Seized with a burning desire to do something useful and significant the editor of this volume decided to ask the country's golf writers to choose the eighteen holes (as numbered) which they believed would make up the best composite golf course the Repubic of Ireland could offer.

Twenty-two golf writers and broadcasters were asked to choose the eighteen holes. Eighteen responded before the publication deadline expired. The plan was for one hole selected to top a chapter with an equivalent number of sections (e.g., the par 5 seventh at the K Club adorns the "In the Swing Chapter" which is divided into five sections). The vagaries of selection have resulted in a course with a par of 70 rather than the classic par 72 format.

I felt rather bad about that until Dermot Gilleece of the *Irish Times* reminded me that a par 70 is the classic USGA format for the US Open!

It was my job to sort through the contributions and identify some consensus. On more than half the holes there were clear or even overwhelming winners (the fifteenth at Portmarnock and the third at Mount Juliet being the best examples). The alternate course (included in the event of any of the originals burning to the ground) consists of the holes which finished second in the nominations.

The final selection is not by any means definitive but I would hazard a guess few would argue with the clear-cut winners (I have indicated the number of votes the winners and alternates secured) and arguments about the rest will be a lot of fun anyway. A similar poll among members of the Irish PGA would be an interesting exercise and might throw up an entirely different result. Nevertheless the "course" is an interesting mix of the venerable (Portmarnock, Ballybunion, Killarney) and the modern (Mount Juliet, the K Club, St Margarets). It also includes most of the accepted "championship" courses around the country (Lahinch being the notable exception – though it has three holes which merit inclusion in the eighteen alternates). There is a good mix of links and parkland courses and a good geographical spread.

The yardages and details of designers are taken, either from club Strokesavers, from cards printed in John Redmond's *Great Golf Courses of Ireland*, Charlie Mulqueen's *Ireland's Top Golf Courses*, Pat Ruddy's *Golfer's Companion* magazine or from course cards saved by this writer as a reminder never to give up the day job . . . All measurements are in yards, from championship tees. Where distances are measured in metres on the card the appliance of higher mathematics was required. I did what all Irish golfers do when confronted by metres . . . I divided by ten and added. Where the architects are concerned those credited may not have been directly responsible for the particular hole but are generally accepted to have laid out the course. Where a course was designed by two or more partners I have used the symbol "&". Where a subsequent architect has redesigned the original concept of another I have used the symbol "/". All clear so far?

Here are the eighteen holes the eighteen journalists involved came up with. (Number of votes secured in brackets.)

1st Killarney (Killeen) (Dr Billy O'Sullivan/Eddie Hackett) 367 yds Par 4 (9)

2nd Ballybunion (Old) (Lionel Hewson/Others) 445 yds Par 4 (11)

3rd Mount Juliet (Jack Nicklaus) 184 yds Par 3 (13)

4th Portmarnock (WC Pickeman/Mungo Park and others) 447 yds Par 4 (10)

5th Royal Dublin (ES Colt) 465 yds Par 4 (8)

6th Killarney (Killeen) (Dr Billy O'Sullivan/Eddie Hackett) 195 yds Par 3 (7)

7th K Club (Arnold Palmer & Ed Seay) 608 yds Par 5 (10)

8th European Club (Pat Ruddy) 412 yds Par 4 (7)

9th County Louth (Baltray) (Tom Simpson) 422 yds Par 4 (6)

Out: 3545 yds Par 35

10th Mount Juliet (Jack Nicklaus) 548 yds Par 5 (6)

11th Ballybunion (Old) (Lionel Hewson/Others) 449 yds Par 4 (9)

12th Tralee (Arnold Palmer & Ed Seay) 448 yds Par 4 (6)

13th The Island (Fred Hawtree & Eddie Hackett and others) 210 yds Par 3 (7)

14th Waterville (Eddie Hackett & John A Mulcahy) 458 yds Par 4 (6)

15th Portmarnock (WC Pickeman/Mungo Park and others) 187 yds Par 3 (15)

16th K Club (Arnold Palmer & Ed Seay) 394 yds Par 4 (6)

17th County Sligo (ES Colt) 455 yds Par 4 (5)

18th St Margarets (Pat Ruddy & Tom Craddock) 458 yds Par 4 (10)

In: 3607 yds Par 35

Total 7152 yds Par 70

ALTERNATE 18 HOLES
1st Lahinch (Old) 387 yds Par 4
2nd Tralee 590 yds Par 5
3rd Waterville 440 yds Par 4
4th Lahinch (Old) 430 yds Par 4
5th Lahinch (Old) 488 yds Par 5
6th Ballybunion (Old) 364 yds Par 4
7th European Club 421 yds Par 4
8th St Margarets 525 yds Par 5
9th Portmarnock 437 yds Par 4
10th Hermitage 142 yds Par 3
11th Waterville 500 yds Par 5
12th County Louth 420 yds Par 4
13th Mount Juliet 438 yds Par 4
14th Portmarnock 386 yds Par 4
15th The Island 558 yds Par 5
16th Carlow 434 yds Par 4
17th Ballybunion 379 yds Par 4
18th Mount Juliet 476 yds Par 4

Should anyone wish to tackle this "course" please keep me informed of the results of your "round" and we can establish a "course record". But I think a legitimate "round" must be played within one calendar year.

And may the Lord have mercy on your (golf) balls!

First Hole: Brain Dead Par 4

Hole: 1st Killarney (Killeen)
Par 4 367 yds
Designer: Dr Billy O'Sullivan/Eddie Hackett

You don't have to be a rocket scientist to be a golfer. In fact the paucity of rocket scientists among golfing ranks may bespeak a certain intellectual dullness amongst members of the fraternity. (A close study of their social attitudes would reinforce this belief.)

The intellectual challenge of poking a hooded 7-iron shot through a gap in the trees may not exercise those convolutions of the brain which are responsible for the production of poetry, quantum theory or even rational thought. And even if it did, those newly excited brain cells would be liable to perish in the clubhouse bar after the round as the golfer regaled the hypnotised assembly with a highly flavoured account of how he had managed to extricate himself from the bushes. His stirring account would be assisted by intermittent calls of "SettemupagainJoe" as the First Armoured Alcohol Brigade assaulted his brain cells.

(NOTE: The reason for the attentive audience has nothing to do with the interest level in our golfer's exploits – all golfers who listen to such dismal anecdotes do so on the understanding that it's their turn next.)

Let us not be too hard on golfers though. Apart from elitism (male and female), snobbery (male and female) and egregious misogyny (male) they are as fine a bunch of people as ever stalked a putt. But they do have their downsides and it is this "dark side of the force" which is recognised in this chapter. However, in keeping with the naïve spirit of childish innocence which otherwise pervades this great game we will begin with a selection of what, in *Private Eye* are known as "Colemanballs". So-called, after the BBC broadcaster David Coleman, who was noted for his malapropisms.

BRICKS

"I have a Mercedes and a Mazda, I only have two hands."
  Jose Maria Olazabal

"I'm so busy I can only play in one tournament at a time."
  Jack Nicklaus

"This is Vincente Fernandez of Argentina. You will notice he walks with a slight limp. This is because he was born with one leg shorter than the other two."
  Roddy Carr doing an RTE commentary for the Carrolls Irish Open

"His future is ahead of him."
  Steve Melnyk's TV comment on Phil Mickelson

Palmer: "Say Tip, do you know where that plaque is?"
Anderson: (His caddy) "Sure I do. It's 250 miles away – at Royal Birkdale!"
  Arnold Palmer at Troon looking for a plaque commemorating an Open winning shot at Birkdale in 1961

"I'm not as bingo, bango, bongo as you think."
  Mac O'Grady, known as Mad Mac, replying to a journalist who asked him if he was crazy

"I know this course is hundreds of years old but I'm not into that."
  Mark Calcavecchia being blasphemous about St Andrews in 1990 (Serves him right that he missed the cut)

"Ninety percent of the game is half mental."
  Unattributed quote

Jacklin: "Hey, Sandy, where are you going?"
Lyle: "To the toilet!"
  Tony Jacklin and Sandy Lyle – a surprise meeting at an airport

"Greg Norman will be the toast of Sandwich tonight."
  BBC Radio Five commentary on Norman's 2nd British Open triumph, in 1993

"How in the world did they ever get that? I've never been to New York in my life."
Sam Snead on being shown a picture of himself in a New York paper

"What did he go out in?"
Sam Snead on being told that Presidential candidate Thomas Dewey was leading in the polls in 1948

"Is that right? How long are decades nowadays?"
Sam Snead on learning that he had won tournaments in six different decades

"This guy looks like a pecker."
John Jacobs on American TV demonstrating his ignorance of American slang

"To Die, best wishes."
Sandy Lyle's autograph on a ball for his good friend, journalist Dai Davies

"I'd give it six out of ten, or 70%."
Lyle again, on being asked to assess his game

"You know, you can't really tell from here whether that's a man or a woman."
Lyle – on seeing a streaker as he stood on the 18th tee prior to winning the 1985 Open at Sandwich – to his caddy Dave Musgrove

"Is that a golf course?"
Lyle on being asked for an assessment of the American junior star "Tiger" Woods

"I've played in Japan. Is that near Asia?"
Fred Couples on being asked had he ever played in Asia

"I just have this feeling somebody's going to be on the other end."
Couples on why he doesn't answer the telephone

"I learn English from American pros. That's why I speak so bad. I call it PGA English."
Roberto di Vicenzo

BOOZE

"The way I hit the ball today, I need to go to the range. Instead, I think I'll go to the bar."
Fuzzy Zoeller

"I have never led the tour in money winnings, but I have many times in alcohol consumption."
Fuzzy Zoeller

"You know what I did here one year? I was so nervous I drank a fifth of rum before I played. I shot the happiest 83 of my life."
Chi Chi Rodriguez at the Masters

"I had six pints of lager over the last nine holes and shot 62 and then downed eight more while I was waiting for a play-off with Brian Waites."
Brian Barnes on the last (so far) of his 15 PGA tour wins, at Dalmahoy in 1981

"Even a year ago I was seeing three balls instead of one when I teed up. Now I only drink water."
Barnes speaking after he had given up booze

"I like to say I was born in the 19th hole – the only one I ever parred."
George Low, US Tour camp follower. More a "presence" than a "hanger-on".

"That poor man exhausted himself. I'd no idea golf was such a strenuous game."
Naïve war hero, Sgt Alvin York, watching wartime pro Lefty Stackhouse (suffering from an outrageous hangover) struggling through a round . . .

"On the practice ground he was hitting his divots further than the balls."
Caddy's comment on Sweden's Michael Krantz suffering from an excess of Guinness during the 1990 Irish Open (He actually fell on his caddy, collapsed again on the first tee and shot an 82)

"I take a handful of pills every morning for congestive heart failure. The doctor said I need to alleviate stress. I figure there's no stress in trying to make a 3-footer. It's when he took me off cigarettes and booze that it almost killed me."
US pro Don January

Player: (On the phone) "Is that Lee Trevino?"
Trevino: "Wait a minute. Let me look in the mirror. (Pause) Yep, it's me all right."
Gary Player and Trevino after a "convivial evening" for Trevino

"If I win here Sunday I won't know it till Thursday."
Lee Trevino

"I told someone to make me a cup of black coffee and put a stiffener in it. I clouted the first drive down the right-hand side of the fairway into the trees and everybody thought I had hit a bad shot. What they didn't know was that my man was standing in the trees with coffee and a hair of the dog . . . I went on to shoot a 68."
Christy O'Connor Sr after a hard night and a mad dash to the first tee during the 1963 Canada Cup

"WC Fields was fond of playing the course sideways with his pal, Oliver Hardy. He liked being in the trees where he could drink without scandalising the natives."
Jim Murray on Fields's membership of the Lakeside club in Los Angeles

"It's no secret. I've been in hospital for drinking too much. I wasn't a hard drinker – I found it easy! I'd drink so much I'd wake up feeling like horse manure. I did everything like it was a mission. I'd drink until I couldn't see straight. If it was an automobile, I can get there faster than you . . . "
John Daly

"Hell, most people would be drunk for two days on what I'd have before dinner."
John Daly

"Some of my best putting displays came when I had a really good buzz from alcohol."
Daly on PWI (Putting While Intoxicated)

"A policeman stopped me once and said, 'Sir, have you been drinking a little?' I said, 'No, I've been drinking a lot.'"
Daly again . . .

"I've had more headaches being sober than ever I had when I drank."
. . . and again . . .

"If I take another drink I'm history. It's a lot easier knowing you can't do something than knowing you shouldn't. I can't."
. . . and yet again, having been taught the error of his ways by the US PGA Tour Commissioner Deane Beman

"Moderation is essential in all things, Madam, but never in my life have I failed to beat a teetotaller."
Harry Vardon rejecting the course of temperance

"They're usually pretty red."
Raymond Floyd when asked the colour of his eyes

"However explicit your instructions to the barman, you will never get a decent martini."
Henry Longhurst on English and Scottish golf clubs

"It's enjoyable. Let's just say I can handle several gallons."
Darren Clarke on his love of Guinness

"He was fond of a regular sip. The Americans dubbed him Henry 'Don't mind if I do' Longhurst, or 'Henry Longthirst'."
Peter Alliss on Henry Longhurst's penchant for the occasional one

BORES AND LOSERS

"I was on the dance floor but I couldn't hear the band."
Chi Chi Rodriguez on losing

"Show me someone who gets angry once in a while, and I'll show you a guy with a killer instinct. Show me a guy walking down the fairway smiling and I'll show you a loser."
Lee Trevino

"The only way we're going to beat this guy is if he signs the wrong scorecard."
Lee Trevino's caddy, Herman Mitchell, on Jack Nicklaus

"My luck is so bad that if I bought a cemetry people would stop dying."
American pro Ed Furgol

"People don't seem to realise how often you have to come in second in order to finish first . . . I've never met a winner who hadn't learned how to be a loser."
Jack Nicklaus

"Second place sucks."
The highly competitive American Ken Green

"He beat me by one hole and, if only I could have saved a stroke or two here and there, I am convinced that he still would have beaten me by one hole."
Henry Longhurst on a match with the great Francis Ouimet

"Competitors take bad breaks and use them to drive themselves just that much harder. Quitters take bad breaks and use them as reasons to give up. It's all a matter of pride."
Nancy Lopez

"The trouble with this game is that they say the good breaks and the bad breaks even up. What they don't tell you is that they don't even up right away."
Johnny Miller

"When I retire, I'm going to get a pair of grey slacks, a white shirt, a striped tie, a blue blazer, a case of dandruff and go stand on the first tee so I can be a USGA official."
Lee Trevino (He was probably fined for saying it)

Journalist: "Well, you can't win 'em all."
Strange: "Why not?"
A young Curtis Strange snarling after failing to repeat his 1974 NCAA title success

"I'm a good loser. Then again I've had more practice at it than virtually anyone else out there."
David Feherty

"One thing that will help keep you calm while playing golf is to remember that nobody gives a damn about your bad golf but you."
Don Herold (And the fourball behind you!)

"Listening to Mize drone on at countless press conferences after that Masters victory was like drowning in Horlicks."
Bill Elliot, Golf Correspondent of the Star

"Andy North . . . has indeed won the US Open twice, in 1978 and 1985. Apart from these triumphs he has achieved little except managing to consistently tie his shoelaces and hoist his pants on the right way round."
Bill Elliot

"Jeff [Sluman] 5'7" of non-explosive dynamite, lists his special interests as the Stock Market and the Tour Policy Board. He probably hasn't discovered crochet yet."
Bill Elliot on the former US PGA Championship winner

"Who cares but yourself and the missus."
The late Tony Lema to a golf bore intent on regaling him with a description of his round

"I would rate Adlai Stevenson and Jack Nicklaus the two most decorous losers to play on the world stage."
Writer and golfer "Laddie" Lucas

BIGOTS

"[Members] have the right to associate or not to associate with whomever we choose . . . we don't discriminate in every other area except the blacks."
Hall Thompson, founder of Shoal Creek Country Club in Alabama, who caused consternation before the 1990 US PGA Championship, leading to a threat to pull the event

"This honest man, Mr Thompson, has exposed the sophisticated layer of deceit and hypocrisy that veils the racism that still exists in our society today."
Rev Joseph Lowery of the Southern Christian Leadership Conference

"Meanwhile Shoal Creek's members are reported to be engaged in a hurry-up search for a black man, any black man, who can both afford the $35,000 initiation fee and tolerate their company. I don't think they'll find him."
Tom Callahan, Washington Post (They did! sixty-six-year-old black, Louis Willie, joined nine days before the PGA Championship.)

"What Lee Trevino has done is take the game out of the country club boardroom and put it in the parking lot where everybody – not just doctors and lawyers but Indian chiefs too – can get at it."
Journalist Curry Kirkpatrick

"A Martian skimming overhead in his saucer would have to conclude that white earthlings hit the ball and black earthlings fetch it, that white men swing the clubs and black men carry them."
John Updike writing about the 1980 Masters

"It looked like a civil rights march out there. People were afraid we were going to steal their hubcaps."
Chi Chi Rodriguez (when partnered by Homero Blancas during the Anderson-Pacific Golf Classic in 1983)

"I'd like to show them that you don't have to get banged up on a football field or be 7'3" to make a living."
Calvin Peete on his example to black sportsmen

"For me a moment of truth came when the club refused to admit a popular Jewish leader for membership. When I heard this, it challenged my values. I made a personal decision to quit without a fanfare. The local papers picked it up, and then pretty soon the national media did. And it has made a difference."

Tom Watson, whose wife, Linda, is Jewish. He quit his membership of Kansas City Country Club where he had learned his golf.

"There are clubs exclusively for Jews and clubs where a Jew could only gain admittance if he arrived on the doorstep with Moshe Dayan at his side supported by a regiment of Israeli paratroopers."

Michael Parkinson during his anti-golf years

"Everybody knew exactly where to find the new 1963 Natal Open champion when officials came to present him with the prize money and the trophy. He was waiting outside the clubhouse because he was a coloured man and therefore, under apartheid laws, prohibited from entering the building. And it was raining."

Gary Player on the treatment meted out to Sewsunker "Papwa" Sewgolum

"I am of the South Africa of Verwoerd and apartheid."

Gary Player in 1965, a statement he later had much cause to regret

"In much of the world, this humbling game is an automatic symbol of capitalist-imperialist oppression; a progressive African novelist, to establish a character as a villain, has only to show him coming off a golf course."

John Updike

"Go home nigger."

Racist taunt screamed at black PGA golfer Charlie Sifford at the Greensboro' Open in South Carolina in the 1960s

Second Hole: Filthy Lucre Par 4

Hole: 2nd Ballybunion (Old)
Par 4 445 yds
Designer: Lionel Hewson & others

Harry Vardon was one of the first victims of golf sponsorship. "The Vardon Flyer", a ball with pimples rather than dimples, was named after him. He was despatched on a 26,000-mile train journey round the USA to promote the ball. He returned with tuberculosis and the ball was soon superseded by technological developments.

Why was this allowed to happen to one of the game's first icons? Because Mike McManager wasn't around, of course. Vardon did not have the benefit of the cigar-smoking agent's deal-making prowess, or of being able to read his book "What They Don't Teach You In The Federal Penitentiary".

McManager would have ensured that the Englishman would never have needed to demean himself by endorsing silly looking golf balls with teenage acne. McManager, with his talent and breadth of vision would have ensured that Vardon was making lateral water hazards full of money without even having to swing a club. Vardon could have retired a millionaire and watched the royalties pour in without ever having had to win any of those puerile Open championships.

How, do I hear you ask? How, indeed! A Mike McManager, at the turn of the century, would have patented the Vardon Overlapping Grip!!! Simple but brilliant. The money would still have been flooding into the Vardon (And McManager) estate to this day. Statistically the overwhelming proportion of golfers (apart from baseball players or those who like their index and little fingers to make love) use the Overlapping Grip, the development of which is ascribed to Vardon. So, every time a player held a club in his or her hand (with possible exemptions on the putting green) Vardon could have expected to receive a royalty. (Whenever *Where Do You Go To My Lovely* is played on a commerical radio station – which it is at least twelve times a day – Peter Sarstedt gets a royalty! Right?)

But Vardon could only have done it with a McManager to see the potential. Isn't it wonderful how times have changed?

MONEY

"Putts get real difficult the day they pass the money out."
Lee Trevino

"I have to win this tournament. My wife bought $50,000 worth of furniture last week. And you should see the house she built around it."
Lee Trevino

"The world's a funny place. When you have no money, no one will do anything for you. If you become successful and pile up enough money to buy anything you want, people deluge you with gifts you don't need and try to do all kinds of things for you."
Lee Trevino

"You can make a lot of money in this game. Just ask my ex-wives. Both of them are so rich that neither of their husbands need to work."
Trevino

"We're not doing too bad, you know. The man who finishes 150th makes $50,000 which is more than most college professors – and that's the way it should be in this world, unless you're too ignorant to see it."
Bobby Joe Grooves (Dan Jenkins's fictional pro)

"The top ten finishers each should get most of the money. This would encourage the rest to work hard. Finishing 20th every week should not guarantee you a good living."
Seve Ballesteros

"Victory is everything. You can spend the money, but you can never spend the memories."
Ken Venturi

"Loaning you money is like sending lettuce by rabbit."
George Low, infamous "hanger-on", to a potential debtor

"You hear guys talk about titles – that's all that's important. They've all got £5 million in their bank accounts. I haven't, so I'm after the money. It's as simple as that."
Mark James speaking in 1989 (He's built up a decent nest egg since then)

"There's so much money, all down the line, that some of 'em don't even drink coffee or a Coke. They say it might make them nervous. Now ain't that something."
Sam Snead

"Sam's got more money buried underground than I ever made on top. He's got gophers in the backyard that subscribe to *Fortune* magazine."
Palmer on Snead's reputed meanness

"Instead of putting money in the bank Sam Snead buries it in tins in his backyard."
American pro, Jimmy Demaret

"Jimmy Demaret started that story and after it got in the papers a few times, I came home one night and found a man with a hoe, a rake and a lantern in my backyard."
Snead on Demaret's quote

"These kids have it mighty soft today. I recently heard one of my members say to his son, 'You're a golf bum. Are you going to be content to spend your life tramping around the golf course?' And the kid said, 'No, Pop, I've been meaning to speak to you about buying me my own golf cart.'"
Sam Snead

"There goes $100,000."
Al Watrous after watching Bobby Jones make a miraculous bunker shot to the 17th at Lytham in the Open. Jones won.

"Harry Vardon's career earnings would be insignificant against the income of one of today's touring caddies."
Peter Dobereiner

21

"Anthony David Lema, the new Open Champion, is really rather a splendid fellow, absolutely in the Hagen tradition of not wanting to be a millionaire but possessed of a strong determination to live like one."
Henry Longhurst writing in 1964 of Tony Lema

"I once played with Henry Ford II and told him, 'You can buy a country, but you can't buy a golf swing. It's not on the shelf.'"
Gene Sarazen

"If you're in the top 20 on Sunday, a birdie will make you twice what a bogey will cost you."
US pro Mark Brooks

"He still owes me a quarter of a million pounds."
Bob Taylor on a teammate who bet him 25p at odds of a million to one that he wouldn't ace the 16th at Hunstanton GC in England, in 1974, for the third consecutive day. He duly holed out with a 6-iron.

"I think right now I'm third in money-winning and first in money-spending."
Tony Lema at the Open in 1964

"Maybe, but I collect the cheques with my right."
Bobby Locke on suggestions that his left hand was the cause of his "weak" grip

"The money involved is enormous and it doesn't look good for millionaire golfers to shrug off a missed putt for a fortune when you realise the putt might have won more than some viewers earn in their whole lifetime."
Frank Nobilo

"I'll take second place everytime. Of course I want to win, but I'm not going to knock second if I don't. The only person who doesn't like runner-up spot is someone who does not like money."
David Feherty

"If I weren't a golfer I would like to be in advertising – lots of punters who wear red specs and pony tails and swan around drinking cups of coffee and making money. That would suit me."
David Feherty

"I figured the man who won the most money was the best."
Woosnam on his drive to top the European money list

"I remember when I didn't have any."
Woosnam explaining his desire to earn as much money as possible on the Pro circuit

"One million dollars a foot."
IMG (Mark McCormack's firm) manager's assessment of Woosnam's worth in 1991 after winning the Masters (the reference being to his height, not his feet)

"I was never good at mathematics but I do understand numbers with a bunch of zeros on the end."
Chi Chi Rodriguez

"Almost certainly the single most influential man in professional sport in the entire world."
Peter Alliss on Mark McCormack

SPONSORS

"Julius Boros would be a bookkeeper in Connecticut; Arnold Palmer would still be in the Coast Guard; and I'd be back in Texas picking cotton."
Trevino on where the pros would be without sponsors

"I've been a test pilot for Foot Joy Forever. I test their $65 alligator models to see if standing in them for long periods of time in a bar brings them any serious harm."
George Low on a unique sponsorship deal

"I wish! These cost me four quid each in Dubai."
Trish Johnson on being asked whether Chanel sponsored the tee shirt she was wearing

"If you don't mind, Mr Crosby, I'd rather have the cash."
Sam Snead to Bing Crosby when he handed him a cheque for winning the 1937 Crosby Pro-Am

"I (also) got a lot of offers of hotel rooms and women, but I could get those on my own."

Sam Snead on the payment of appearance money by sponsors in the USA before it was banned in the 1950s

"I felt everybody was against me and I became scared of people. I felt like I was in a restaurant, alone, and people whom I didn't know were talking about me."

Seve Ballesteros talking about his "appearance money" row with the European tour in 1981

"When Jack Nicklaus builds a golf course and promises to play in the first tournament held on it, his design fee goes up from $1.5 million to $1.6 million."

Bernhard Langer suggesting that there are different ways of paying appearance money in the USA

"I don't believe a great golfer gives less of an effort because he got appearance money, and I don't believe the appearance money will be added to the purse if you ban it."

David Leadbetter

"I just signed to do commercials for a mattress company and fulfilled my life's ambition. I'll get paid for lying down."

Lee Trevino

"The guys out there are starting to look like race car drivers."

Tom Weiskopf on sponsorship logos

"My chief regret was that I hadn't signed up with a good Chinese laundry and a nationwide we-pick-it-up-anywhere dry cleaning service."

Jack Nicklaus on the sponsors he didn't have in his early days on the tour

"Nobody really knows what it is like to play golf for money until you haven't got it . . . sometimes we had to win money to get out of town, to pay the hotel bill. When we couldn't win enough, we'd sneak down the fire escapes. Later, when we won some, we'd send the hotel a money order. Nowadays all the pros got sponsors.

Sponsors for chrissake! You know who my sponsors were? Them ladders. That's who. Them lousy ladders."
Lloyd Mangrum

"I feel that if there are no entertainers . . . then there will be no sponsors. And if there are no sponsors, then there is no tour. We must go our own way, without the flaxen-haired, robot figures bred on the US circuit."
Ronan Rafferty speaking in 1984

"There are some things I've never liked over there, like those sponsors who say 'It's great to have you in our tournament', and you feel like replying 'If it's so great, why aren't I in the pro-am?'"
Faldo on competing in the US after his first British Open triumph

"People have to eat and, presumably, drink, but the necessity of sponsoring golf tournaments is not so readily apparent."
BBC commentator Bruce Critchley on the fact that food, drink and golf tournament sponsorship seemed to be the only growth areas of the 1990s

"Don't ever set up one of those for me again, I felt like a prostitute."
Tony Jacklin to Mark McCormack after playing with a different fourball on each of 18 holes during a "corporate" day

"I'm very near the end now. I've never been a religious man, but I know that you and I will meet again, many years from now, in another place. The one good thing about me going first is that at least it will afford me the opportunity of finding the sponsor's hospitality room."
Henry Longhurst's last conversation with Peter Alliss before he died

HUSTLERS

"The more competent a player, the smaller the stake that contents him. It is only when you get down into the submerged tenth of the golfing world that you find the big gambling."
PG Wodehouse

"For Chrissakes my caddy can beat you."
Prelude to a Titanic Thompson hustle. His caddy was future pro Ky Laffoon.

"I come from a different era. I started out shining shoes, giving lessons, selling 10E shoes to some guy who wears 12C, and making him like it."
Lee Trevino

"You don't know what pressure is until you play for five bucks with only two in your pocket."
Lee Trevino

"A hustler he is not and a hustler he has never been. To hustle is to deceive. Lee was just there with his game and everybody knew it."
Fellow pro Arnold Salinas on Lee Trevino

"Put me on a putting green in Miami and I'll kill more tourists than the Fountainbleau."
George Low on his speciality

"There ain't no use hanging round a broke, because nothing falls off."
George Low

"Driving your getaway car is the best job in golf."
George Low to Mark McCormack

"I shall have to admit, in all modesty, that I'm probably the greatest putter who ever lived. At least I'll try anyone for a nominal fee."
George Low

"You can drop the limp now!"
Lionel Platts to Royal Dublin amateur Noel O'Neill after he and Christy O'Connor Sr had taken a lot of money from Platts and Hedley Muscroft. O'Neill had a bad leg.

"I'm expecting a wire from the Vatican any day, asking for a review of my handicap."
Fr John Durkin after winning the 1971 Crosby Pro-Am with Lou Graham. He was playing off an exceptionally generous 17.

"I've always argued that we ought to play right down the middle of Saigon if the price was right."
   Frank Beard in 1970 (It would be a good deal safer today)

"It must be the economy. Everybody wants to play for twosies and fivesies now. I used to play a $25 Nassau against everybody in a group. It was like pickin' up corn."
   Sam Snead at 82, still able to shoot ten strokes below his age

"Over the years I've studied habits of golfers. I know what to look for. Watch their eyes. Fear shows up when there is an enlargement of the pupils. Big pupils lead to big scores."
   Sam Snead

"Back horses or go down to Throgmorton Street and try to take it away from the Rothschilds, and I will applaud you as a shrewd and cautious financier. But to bet at golf is pure gambling."
   PG Wodehouse's "The Oldest Member"

"The fine fabric of golf is also frequently tugged to the ripping point by golfers who are not above deliberately "using" the social relationships the game affords as their chief tactic for winning their matches . . . it is easy in golf. Your opponent is always within conversational range."
   The great golf writer Herbert Warren Wind on gamesmanship

"If you find yourself being outplayed by the excellent iron approaches of your adversary, it is sometimes a good plan to say to him, in a tone of friendly interest, 'Really you are playing your iron wonderfully well today – better than I ever saw you play it before. Can you account for it in any way?' . . . only after a time will people stop playing with you."
   Writer Horace Hutchinson

"Never bet with anyone you meet on the first tee who has a deep suntan, a 1-iron in his bag and squinty eyes."
   Dave Marr, former pro and commentator

"Some guys get so nervous playing for their own money, the greens don't need fertilising for a year."
   Dave Hill

"They play for big bucks at private clubs, too, but there's a difference. They can afford to lose."
Hale Irwin

"One reward golf has given me, and I shall always be thankful for it, is introducing me to some of the world's most picturesque, tireless and bald-faced liars."
American humourist Ring Lardner

SNOBS

"I played Royal Foxshire and they made me wear a suit and tie . . . in the shower. You can't get a starting time on Sunday unless you've been knighted."
Bob Hope

"Trevino doesn't like Augusta because he thinks they don't like him."
Bill Elliot, journalist, reflecting on the membership of Augusta National

"There are clubs in England and Scotland where you are made to feel guilty for neglecting to wear a sign reading 'Leper' round your neck and to signal your approach by ringing a hand bell. That level of pompous assery is unthinkable in Ireland."
Peter Dobereiner (Don't be so sure!)

"Joining a golf club is almost as hard as becoming a mason, though once you're in, if you wear plus-fours, as many golfers still do, it saves pulling up a trouser leg."
British journalist Alex Spillius

"Their lordships always repair to their castles when they wish to bathe, Sir."
A steward in the St Andrews locker room informing American pro Ed Furgol that there were no showers

"The galleries over there were wonderful, but the club members' attitudes were a little sticky. In 1937 we pros were allowed in the clubhouse, but not our wives. Except the last day. The weather was so bad, they finally relented and let them in."
Byron Nelson on why many American pros were reluctant to play in the British Open

"It is said eligibility for membership is a Hoover button, a home in Pasadena and proof-positive that you never had an actor in the family. Once, when a member proposed Jimmy Roosevelt for membership, they not only blackballed Roosevelt, they kicked out the member."

Golf columnist Jim Murray on the exclusive LA Country Club

"The club is open. There is no bar as to who should join the club. We've got Dr Shah, we've got a couple of coloured members. There's no bar, so long as you've got a reasonable income."

Vice-captain of Northwood Golf Club in England on Channel 4's "Cutting Edge" programme, from which the club emerged with little credit

"We showed the film to almost everyone who was in it a week before it was broadcast and they seemed pretty pleased about it. They all agreed it showed Northwood as it was that autumn."

Kate Woods, TV director of the programme

"I think after this we have to make a clean start and let us hope we can find some more intelligent people to put on the board."

Preston Lockwood, actor and Northwood club member

"I remember going to a British Open in Scotland (I'm not going to say which course) and we weren't allowed into the clubhouse, women just weren't allowed in. The ladies toilet was on the side of the clubhouse and we went in there, I remember standing in the rain outside."

Mary O'Connor, wife of Christy Sr

"To St Andrews, where we breathe an atmosphere of pure golf, there comes occasionally some darkened man, to whom the game is unknown. If he is a distinguished stranger, pains are usually taken to enlighten him . . . If he is an undistinguished stranger, he is, of course, tabooed at once and handed over to croquet and the ladies, if they will have him."

Lord Moncrieff of Tulliebole

"I could see that Muirfield was empty. I thought the reason they wouldn't let us play was because they were having a competition or something, but there wasn't a soul on it."

Payne Stewart playing Gullane after having been turned away from Muirfield

"I'm aware of stories that have been told for years. I'm aware of how nervous some of them acted. I'm not convinced that any of the shaking was genuine at all. They acted the way they thought I expected them to act."

Captain PWT (Paddy) Hanmer, the secretary of Muirfield, renowned for showing the gate to many who had the effrontery to ask to be allowed play Muirfield, talking to Michael Bamberger

Third Hole: Monstrous Regimen Par 3

Hole: 3rd Mount Juliet
Par 3 184 yds
Designer: Jack Nicklaus

Women complain, with complete justification, about the second-class treatment meted out to them in the vast majority of golf clubs. But they should spare a thought for one of the first women golfers and the fate which befell her. Mary Queen of Scots defied convention and challenged the stranglehold of the Royal and Ancient back in the sixteenth century and was thwarted in her attempt to strike a blow for women. She suffered the ultimate fate for her brave but futile campaign, she died for her religion.

Her consistent refusal to give way to Saturday men's fourballs at her local Edinburgh club, her insistence on exercising her voting rights as Honorary Patron, and her campaign for full membership for women, marked her down in the eyes of the Committee, and society in general, as a bare downhill lie. The fact that she could take on any of the members of that Committee on even terms and hammer them at the game, marked her down as a slick undulating green. A contemporary poem puts it well "Gang crank aye ye mair ye Quane y Scotts/Bate ye Committay wi'out ye schotts".

Her exalted position precluded a simple expulsion from the club so the aid of her croquet-playing cousin, Queen Elizabeth, was enlisted. The rest is history. Mary Queen of Scots, far from fleeing south to escape the wrath of an angry nation was kidnapped and transported to England while trying to extricate herself from a St Andrews pot bunker. Armed only with an old-fashioned wedge she had nothing with which to defend herself.

Her execution had nothing to do with her cleaving to the Roman Catholic religion but her refusal to renounce golf. Contemporary documents are supposed to refer to her "wilful and perverse adherence to the Roman See", however a cursory glance at the relevant document (Scottish Public Record Office CO 4467/34/S) will reveal the cringe-making error which generations of craven historians have colluded in perpetuating, until now. The document, written in an opaque scrawl, quite clearly refers to her "wilful and perverse adherence to the Forward Tee."

Plucky to the last, before she fell victim to the axe, she pointed out to the executioner that his grip on the implement was far too tight for a comfortable backswing and that the number of knuckles on display in the address position would lead to an opening of the face of the axe and a probable slice. And so it proved!

WOMEN PROS

"I can beat any two players in this tournament by myself. If I need any help I'll let you know."
Mildred "Babe" Didrikson Zaharias, famous American player, to a fourball partner

"The little white ball won't move until you hit it, and there's nothing you can do after it has gone."
"Babe" Zaharias

"It's a hard way to make an easy living."
Joyce Kazmierski on the Women's Tour

"If it weren't for golf I'd be waiting on this table instead of sitting at it."
Judy Rankin, American golfer and commentator

Q: "Are you nervous?"
Mann: "No, but my ball must be."
Carol Mann after her ball blew off the tee

"When I go out in the first round and my heart beats, I chuckle and say, 'Hey Muffin, it's only Thursday. Your heart's not supposed to beat until Sunday.'"
American pro Muffin Spencer-Devlin

"You could put any one of us on the European side and make it better. But the only Europeans who could help us are Laura Davies and Liselotte Neumann."
American team member Beth Daniel prior to the 1992 Solheim Cup, which Europe won

"I think they must be in shock. I know I am."
European Solheim Cup-winning captain Mickey Walker talking about the American team

"Let's just say that your players behave very differently to how they do when they are in the States."
American team member Juli Inkster on the tension between the sides

"I've quit worrying about poor shots. I just tell myself, 'Relax Bozo. If you can't have fun you shouldn't be out here.'"
Patty Sheehan

"It wasn't much fun being an amateur. I got tired of polishing the silverware."
Patty Sheehan

"It's nice to have the opportunity to play for so much money, but it's nicer to win it."
Patty Sheehan

"I can't make birdies from somebody's garden."
Laura Davies during a bout of wildness off the tee

"Deep down I have this feeling that I am making a quick getaway from trouble."
Laura Davies on why her play speeds up when she's doing badly

"She's not a contender for Sylph of the Year."
A description of Davies, attributed to fellow pro Muffin Spencer-Devlin, who denies having said it

"She's the 'Gazza' of golf."
Colin Snape, former WPGET (European Women's Tour) tour director on (we presume) Davies's abundant talent

"The LPGA needs a player who looks like Farah Fawcett and plays like Jack Nicklaus. Instead they've got players who look like Jack Nicklaus and play like Farah Fawcett."
(Wisely) Unattributed quote on LPGA Tour in USA

"The cameras affect my game. They make me nervous. I would rather make my money in front of nobody."
American pro Betsy King

"Look like a woman and play like a man."
"Pin-up" pro Jan Stephenson's recipe for success in the Women's Pro Tour

"I love to sweat and heave and breathe and hurt and burn and get dirty."
Jan Stephenson (Who always looks like she's just had a shower)

"There are plenty of cute girls who can play. They should have more tournaments and more money. Someone is not doing a selling job."
Jan Stephenson advancing the cause of feminism while analysing the ills of the WPGET

"I'll take a two stroke penalty, but I'll be damned if I'll play it where it lays."
Elain Johnson, a Canadian amateur, after achieving the difficult feat of hitting her ball into her bra

"If you told her to do something it was almost certain she would do exactly the opposite."
Gordon Severson, US College coach of Sweden's Helen Alfredsson

"She's nuts."
Fellow pro Meg Mallon on Helen Alfredsson

"She's a lunatic."
Laura Davies on Helen Alfredsson

"I'm a very restless person. I had two weeks off in the summer and I tried to just sit by the pool. In half an hour I was going crazy."
Helen Alfredsson

"That putt was so good I could feel the baby applauding."
Donna White, seven months pregnant

"I'll never be another Nancy."
Beth Daniel on Nancy Lopez

"I'm a golfer not a movie star. I come across on first impression like a jerk, stuck-up, really a cold fish."
Beth Daniel on herself

"The sun don't shine on the same dog's behind every time."
Beth Daniel rationalising not winning every week

"She hits shots that just make you tingle."
Daniel's caddy Dee Darden

"If she missed a shot she said something stronger than 'darn', and she'd stick a club in the ground or bounce one off her caddy and roar like Tugboat Annie. In other words if she could play like a man she could act like one too."
Barry McDermott, American writer, on Daniel's legendary temper

"Betsy King is going for her third straight Open victory, but nobody seems to care. When Curtis Strange was going for his third straight, that's all you guys wrote about for a month."
Patty Sheehan in 1991

"I started in engineering and switched to business for my major. If I had stayed for my junior year, I'd have had to switch to basket weaving. It was getting tough."
Nancy Lopez, American pro, on the college system

"I didn't like being fat, and that's exactly what I was – fat! I used to say it was because I was big-boned, but I knew better."
Nancy Lopez

"A set of cosmetically-aided girls, whose bodily curves embellished their golf swings and camouflaged the resolve by which their games (if they were successful) were sustained."
"Laddie" Lucas on women pros

"I'm not concerned about getting in the record books. A good obituary doesn't exactly excite me."
  Joanne Carner

WOMEN ON MEN

"Most tournament professionals think real life is playing golf all day on perfect courses for millions of dollars. Real life is poor people who can't afford to eat."
  US pro Hollis Stacy

"I am a widow, though a wife,
My husband's lost to me;
I seldom see his face at all,
He's joined the BGC [Belfast Golf Club]
His talk is all of drives and putts,
Of holing out in four,
Of bunkers, hazards, mashie shots,
And what he calls his score.
His purse grows leaner every day,
His golf bag fuller grows;
How many balls he's bought
He never will disclose.
I'll join the club myself; and play
When he is out to work;
Dusting and darning, cookery
And washing day I'll shirk.
I'll be home at dinner time
And in my usual seat,
And feed my truant husband well
On excellent tinned meat."
  Poem in the Belfast Newsletter *in 1905*

"I'm going to sleep with my putter tonight. My husband, Don, is going to have to sleep in the other bed."
  US pro Joanne Carner after a hot putting round

"Look at him! When I married him he was a Greek God. Now he's a big fat Greek."
  "Babe" Didrikson Zaharias on her husband

"Rollo is exceedingly good at golf. He scores more than 120 every time, while Mr Burns, who is supposed to be one of the best players in the club, seldom manages to reach 80."
PG Wodehouse's "Mrs Podmarsh" referring to her son Rollo

"I thought I had hit someone else's ball. Then I looked closer at the ball and read the red print. It said 'Marry me?!!!' . . . Mike said if I'd hit the ball out of bounds that would have meant the answer was no."
Carmen Minning on the unique way her boyfriend, Mike Warfield, found of proposing

"You're getting so bad you can start hiding your own Easter eggs."
Claudia Trevino to Lee on his habit of forgetfulness

"I was worried about the people behind me getting mad because we would play so slow."
Ms Karen Disabella explaining why she aced the first ever golf hole she played, in 1984

"He quit playing when I started outdriving him."
Big-hitting Joanne Carner on her husband

"All those gentlemanly rools, why, they're the proper rools of affection – all the waitin' and oohin' and ahin' o'er yer shots, all the talk o' this one's drive and that one's putt and the other one's gorgeous swing – what is it all but love? Men lovin' men, that's what golf is."
"Agatha MacNaughton" in Michael Murphy's novel, Golf in the Kingdom

"A game for children with water on the brain who weren't athletic enough to play Animal Grab."
A fictional female view of the game as expressed by PG Wodehouse

"Are you a member?"
One of a foursome of ladies shouting after a man "streaking" across the exclusive Effingham course in London

"Well it just goes to show what we've been saying all along. That all the good-looking professional golfers are on the ladies' tour."
Jan Stephenson after half a dozen male pros (including Payne Stewart and Greg Norman) did "beefcake" shots for Golf *Magazine*

"Hit it in the water again!"
Female fans to Ian Baker-Finch after he'd played a ball out of the water on the previous hole in his boxer shorts

"I may not be the prettiest girl in the world, but I'd like to see Bo Derek rate a "10" after playing 18 holes in 100-degree heat."
Jan Stephenson after a male journalist had rated her at "6"

"I have been moved from a bench at Little Aston golf club in the Midlands, because I was sitting outside the window of the Men's bar."
Journalist Liz Kahn

"Women Who Seek Equality With Men Lack Ambition"
Bumper sticker seen on Patty Sheehan's car

"There's one woman in Palm Springs who embarrasses me half to death – she's always yelling these little endearments, 'darling', 'lover-boy', 'sweetie'. I come down the fairway thinking about my next shot and I suddenly hear her bellow out of the gallery, 'Go lover!' It's not the best thing for your concentration."
Arnold Palmer talking to George Plimpton

"'What fun is there in putting a wee ball?' Mrs Hogg said. 'I don't know what it is about Scotsmen, but they're never happy unless they're playing with their balls. And now women are as bad. They must be after balls the whole time too.'"
Fred Urquhart in his story "Miss Hogg and Miss Cairns"

"After all, golf is only a game."
The naïve Millicent in the PG Wodehouse short story "The Clicking of Cuthbert"

"Women say these things from time to time. It doesn't mean that there is any kink in their character. They simply don't realise what they are saying."
The response of Wodehouse to the above solecism

MEN ON WOMEN

"You women want equality, but you'll never get it because women are inferior to men in all sorts of ways – physically, intellectually, and morally. There are exceptions, but on the whole women are inferior to men."
Seve Ballesteros in the Spanish newspaper El Pais

"Golf may have driven more people crazy than women."
Dan Jenkins

"It is still disappointingly cool here for those who like to witness the female form."
TV commentator Ben Wright covering a tournament for CBS

"If they choose to play at times when male golfers are feeding or resting, no one can object."
Local convention regarding women golfers at St Andrews

"I noticed a lady in the clubhouse at the weekend. I urge the Secretary to see that this does not happen again."
An entry in the complaints book of the Worcestershire Golf Club in England

Reporter: "I understand you have four girlfriends!"
Ballesteros: (Tongue in cheek) "I don't know, maybe more. It is very boring when you play the same course every day."

"Shirt-tail hanging out, hair blowing in the wind, dragging on a cigarette. That's sex appeal."
Arnold Palmer on US pro Hollis Stacy

"Once, with Col St Leger Moore, I was on a green behind the musketry range. A bullet sang between us, we found out it was Ladies' Day."
Member of Curragh Golf Club (It was actually Ladies' Day on the rifle range!)

"Call every woman 'Sugar' and you can't go wrong."
Walter Hagen

"It is my experience, or rather I have observed it to be other people's, that women on these trips are an encumbrance equivalent roughly to conceding two shots per round."
Henry Longhurst, in 1937, writing about the fact that six American wives travelled with their Ryder Cup team

"Although we are told nothing about it, there can be little doubt that one of Job's chief trials was that his wife insisted on playing golf with him."
PG Wodehouse's "The Oldest Member"

"Problems were first noticed last summer with the ladies wearing round neck tops. When they bent down it was putting the men off their putts."
Chairman of Saltford Golf Club, Jack Champion, on women golfers not buttoning their blouses

"Three things are as unfathomable as they are fascinating to the masculine mind: metaphysics, golf and the feminine heart."
A Haultain (1908)

"I had this prejudice against the British, until I discovered that fifty per cent of them were female."
Ray Floyd

"Dogs on a golf course, like education, the death penalty, contraception and women wearing trousers in the dining-room, is an issue which divides."
"Laddie" Lucas

"Alaska would be an ideal place for courses – mighty few trees and damn few ladies' foursomes."
American writer Rex Lardner

"I fail to understand how women can turn up at nine o'clock in the morning and play golf. I know my wife couldn't. She's got to get the breakfast."
A male member of the Northwood Golf club in Britain, talking about lady members, as heard on a Channel 4 TV programme

Fourth Hole: Majors Par 4

Hole: 4th Portmarnock
Par 4 447 yds
Designer: WC Pickeman/Mungo Park & others

The US Masters may be the youngest of the four major golf championships but it has long since overtaken its three rivals in a number of respects. It is like an examination which, although its contents are well known, can be sat by generation after generation of students. Its association with one venue is its strength. There is no US Masters rota of courses. The Masters is Augusta, Augusta is the Masters. The students who undertake the examination annually, including those who have already passed with honours, know there are many potential answers to the questions set by the Augusta course.

Why is the Masters unique? Because it poses a very specific challenge. If you don't draw the ball well off the tee you might as well stay at home. If you are long but erratic off the tee you will not be punished by the type of punitive rough the US Golf Association breeds in its laboratories to torture the wayward at the US Open. If you can't handle the glacial Augusta greens take a week off and practise for the Heritage Classic. (If you want to prepare for the Augusta putting surfaces just stand on your coffee table, set it at a rakish angle and put a Wavin pipe under the lip.)

The Masters lacks the history and tradition of the British Open, which has its own ambience and uniqueness and which poses an entirely different set of questions to the golf student. But Augusta has managed to defy the American inferiority complex which only seems to emerge when confronted by reminders of their infant status. It may be the natural arrogance of its Southern connections (less than admirable when it teeters over into racism and elitism) which seems to have welded decades of tradition to a framework which is barely 60 years old.

It may be the pervasive spirit of Robert Tyre Jones Jr, founder of the Masters, which gives the event its cachet. Granted it has no Vardon, Braid or even Hagen on its roll of honour but Jones, the greatest amateur, is the link to Valhalla.

How many Masters champions are never heard of again? As against the US Open which is often won by an artisan, a journeyman, a plasterer who gets to fill in a crack in the roof of the Sistine Chapel. How many potential British Open winners have been gutted by a bizarre bounce on a brown, concrete fairway? Who can name the last five winners of the US Open-wannabe, the PGA Championship?

And where else would they put blue dye in the water so that it looks convincing on TV and spray the magnolias to assist their natural colour? They try to think of everything at the Masters.

US MASTERS

"I've never been to heaven and, thinking back on my life, I probably won't get a chance to go. I guess the Masters is as close as I'm going to get."

Fuzzy Zoeller

"There is absolutely nothing humorous at the Masters. Here, small dogs do not bark and babies do not cry."

Gary Player

"You don't come here to find your game. You come here because you've got one."

Gene Sarazen

"When I saw it, Augusta gave me a very familiar feeling. These were my trees, my colour of green, and I said to myself, 'Seve, one day you will win this tournament.'"

Seve Ballesteros

"The Masters is more like a vast Edwardian garden party than a golf tournament."

Alistair Cooke

"It's like being on another planet for a week."
Fuzzy Zoeller on not being invited to the Masters

"If you get around it in par you believe a little bit more in God."
Dave Marr on Amen Corner

"As a 'mystique' of Augusta has developed, so has a resentful clique of people who feel uncomfortable at a national sports event that conspicuously fails to reproduce the atmosphere of the Superbowl. The mystique and the resentment of it are both nonsense."
Alistair Cooke

"Once I saw the sign saying 'Positively No Admittance' and having to wear about 5,000 badges just to get through the gates, I hated the place. Mind you, I was blacked up at the time so maybe that explains it."
British satirist Peter Cook on the elitism (and closet racism) not too far from the surface of the Masters

"I'll probably never win here unless they put the pins on the tees and the tees on the greens."
Lee Trevino on being a fader on a course which requires draw on all but two holes

Reporter: "Lee, what does playing in the Masters mean to you?"
Trevino: "When I play in the Masters I know that I'm going to have the weekend off."
Trevino, never a great fan of the tournament

"The tournament brass will stop at nothing to keep Arnie happy. He left the 11th fairway one year to go into the woods and relieve himself. The next year a permanent rest room had been built on the spot."
Dave Hill on Palmer at the Masters

"If this was any other tournament but the Masters, I'd have shot 66. But I was choking out there. That green coat plays castanets with your knees."
Chi Chi Rodriguez

"You can't see all the way back to the 13th tee behind the 12th green. That's because they got a Delta Airlines counter back there. After you take your triple bogey on the 12th, you just go back there and say, 'I'd like a one-way ticket back home on Friday night because I just missed the cut.'"

Ken Venturi on the perils of the 12th

"Green grass, green grandstands, green concession stalls, green paper cups, green folding chairs and visors for sale, green and white ropes, green topped Georgia pines . . . If justice were poetic, Hubert Green would win it every year."

Novelist John Updike

"You never can tell, there may be another, easier way to the green."

Jack Nicklaus on the 9th tee watching his ball heading over pine trees destined for the 1st fairway

"My, even the fairways are fast."

Byron Nelson

"My pants legs were flapping on the first tee. Then I looked over at the trees. They were dead still. No wind at all."

American amateur, Vinnie Giles, playing for the first time

"I start choking as soon as I drive up Magnolia Lane."

Gary Player

"I get so sentimental and starry-eyed when I get here that I can't play. Sometimes I wish it all didn't get to me so much."

1984 winner Ben Crenshaw

"This is the only course I know where you choke when you come in the gate."

Lionel Hebert

"I get so jazzed up. My putting just can't stand the pressure of the first round. After I miss my first twelve 3-footers, I recover from the initial blow. By then I'm out of the tournament."

Johnny Miller

"Augusta brings out the wierdness in all of us. The back nine on the final day is a unique situation. The pressure is difficult to describe."
Tom Watson

"For an amatuer, standing on the first hole at the Masters is the ultimate laxative."
Former British Amateur Champion Trevor Homer

"I would insist on cooking it myself and then poison every past champion, so making it easier to win the tournament."
David Feherty on his "fantasy" Champion's Dinner menu

"Mister Gene, you got to hit a 3-wood if you want to clear that water."
Sarazen's caddy just before he took a 4-wood for an albatross at the 1935 Masters

"Hey, hurry up Gene, I got a date tonight."
Walter Hagen to Sarazen before his "miracle" shot

"When I reached the green, the boy reporting the scores to the master scoreboard via telephone was trying to make it clear that Sarazen had got a two at the 15th. The operator on the master scoreboard kept telling him that he was mixed up and obviously meant to report a two on the 16th, the par 3."
Gene Sarazen on the reaction to his albatross on the 15th in 1935

"If this guy wins the Masters, he'll set golf back 50 years."
Cary Middlecoff on Billy Joe Patton, the amateur with the inelegant swing, who challenged in 1954

"I think maybe I make a few friends. That means more than money. What is money, anyway?"
Roberto di Vicenzo, who signed for a wrong card in 1968 and lost by a shot

"On the 15th hole I started thinking about the green jacket. They gave it to Charles Coody."
Johnny Miller, who finished second in 1971

"Seve, I want to tell you something. Those people don't think I can win. You watch, I'll show them."
Gary Player to Seve about the Augusta fans in 1978. He did too!

"I think maybe Player likes to think people are against him so he can fight harder. I'm like that. The more against you are the crowd, the more you want to prove something."
Seve in 1978

"I never had a thought the whole week. I figured my caddy knew the course a whole lot better than me, so I just put out my hand and played whatever club he put in it. The guys who come down here once a year and try to get smart with Mr Jones's course are the dumb ones."
Fuzzy Zoeller, who won in 1979, on his first appearance

"Nice drive. Would you like to play through?"
An acid David Graham to Seve during the 1980 Masters after the Spaniard had hooked his drive on the 17th, onto the 7th green

"Those guys don't intimidate me. I can beat them."
Jodie Mudd, third round leader in 1983, shot a final round 86

"I ran into a fellow I used to know out there."
Jack Nicklaus in 1986 talking about his good form. He won.

"They were all like a bunch of schoolkids peering at it, moving it around with their forks and glancing round the table. Finally, they looked at me and asked, 'What is it?' I told them it was just spicy beef."
Sandy Lyle, who ordered haggis for the 1989 Champion's Dinner

"The slums of Chicago are full of first round leaders."
Peter Jacobsen, who had shot a 67, on Mike Donald's first round 64 in 1989 (Donald shot a second round 82 – the biggest shot differential between a first and second round in Masters history)

"I thought, 'this is for the marbles, so hit it firm.' I just didn't line the putter up right . . . I did not feel under any pressure. I missed the putt, but it had nothing to do with pressure."
Scott Hoch on his missed 20th play-off putt, on the 10th, to win the Masters in 1989. Nick Faldo beat him on the 11th green.

"I just wanted it to be over with, I wanted to know the result."
Woosnam on the last six holes of the 1991 Masters

"What I learned from last year was patience. My temper is improving, little by little. Before I used to lose my head quickly. Now I will lose my head slowly."
Jose Maria Olazabal, on the experience he gained in finishing second to Woosnam in 1991

"Next year I'll play with earplugs."
Australian Craig Parry on the partisanship of the Augusta fans in 1992

"Yeah, it's the longest relationship I've ever had."
John Daly on being paired with Ian Woosnam for all four rounds of the 1994 Masters (and a total of twelve rounds in 10 months)

"John is getting like one of the family. I wouldn't be surprised to see him coming to us on holiday."
Woosnam's wife Glendryth

"I'll probably put it up on a shelf at home to keep the kids and the dog away from it. That way it'll probably be safe for a while."
Jeff Maggert on the ball he used to shoot the first ever Masters albatross on the 13th in 1994

US OPEN

"We're not trying to humiliate the greatest players in the world, we're trying to identify them."
Frank Tatum, USGA President, on USGA courses

"Nobody wins the US Open, it wins you."
American pro Dr Cary Middlecoff, winner in 1949 and 1956

"The US Open flag eliminates a lot of players. Some players just weren't meant to win the US Open. Quite often a lot of them know it."
Jack Nicklaus

"The National Football League doesn't make the field 200 yards long just because it's Superbowl. The National Basketball Association doesn't raise the baskets to 11 feet for the Championship Series. But this week at the US Open . . . the USGA will have the rough deeper than an elephant's eye, the greens slick as Telly Savalas's head and the fairways as narrow as a supermarket aisle."

US journalist Tim Rosaforte

"If the Masters is an offensive show, the US Open is the greatest defensive test in golf."

Peter Jacobsen

"If the USGA could put a lake in the middle of every green, they would."

Dave Stockton

"Why don't they ever ask some of the pros for advice. They are only in the golf tournament business as a hobby. This is our life."

Hale Irwin on the USGA and their way of setting up courses for the US Open

"Every drive in the Open becomes an adventure."

Frank Haningan, USGA official

"I'm going for the flag today. I'm gonna be a firecracker out there. I'm gonna be so hot they're gonna be playing on brown fairways tomorrow."

Chi Chi Rodriguez

"Any player can win the US Open, but it takes a helluva player to win two."

Walter Hagen speaking before anyone had ever heard of Andy North

"The Open was easier to win when I started. Now they're setting up the courses so it's no longer any fun to play."

Sam Snead on the only Major he's never won

"If you don't win the Open there's a gap in your record."

Gene Sarazen

"If I'd murdered someone I'd have lived it down sooner than the '39 Open."

Snead on taking an 8 at the 18th at the Philadelphia Golf Club to lose the 1939 US Open

"The fairways were so narrow you had to walk down them single file."

Cary Middlecof, on the 1951 Open at Oakland Hills, won by Ben Hogan

"I'm glad I've brought the monster to its knees."

Hogan on Oakland Hills in 1951

"If I had to play that golf course every week, I'd get another business."

Hogan's subsequent reaction to the course, recollected in tranquility

"It had grass in it that looked like it was three feet deep. If you got in there, you might never be found again. I mean it was the kind of place where you hunted buffalo – not par."

Palmer on the first at Cherry Hills in Denver where he won the 1960 US Open

"Gradually I settled down and merely walked on air."

Nicklaus's reaction to winning his first US Open in 1962 at Oakmont

"Am I far enough ahead that I can choke and still win?"

Trevino to fans during the last round of his 1968 win at Oak Hill, his first major victory

"I may buy the Alamo and give it back to Mexico."

Lee Trevino when asked what he would do with his winnings in 1968

"Well I'm not going to buy this place. It doesn't have indoor plumbing."

Trevino after actually visiting the Alamo

"What does it matter who Orville Moody is? At least he brought the title back to America."
Dave Marr (Moody succeeded Trevino as champion in 1969)

"Eighty acres of corn and a few cows."
Bob Rosburg on what Hazeltine needed in 1970 to bring it up to scratch

"Tempo."
The message Tom Weiskopf left in Tony Jacklin's locker before the final round of the 1970 US Open, which Jacklin won in a canter

"To me, the USGA is out for one thing: To get us mad and find out who can keep his cool."
George Archer, who at the 1972 Open at Pebble Beach got so mad he deliberately hit a succession of balls into the Pacific Ocean

"They tried to preserve their almighty power – or almighty par. They really made a joke out of it."
Nicklaus on the so-called "Massacre at Winged Foot", the 1974 US Open, won by Hale Irwin on 7 over par

"When I was walking down the fairway, I saw a bunch of USGA guys down on their hands and knees parting the rough trying to find my ball. I knew I was in trouble.
Jim Colbert at Winged Foot in 1974

"It couldn't have been too bad a lie. I could still see your knees."
Hubert Green to Lanny Wadkins at the same venue

"All of a sudden I'm an expert on everything. Interviewers want your opinion of golf, foreign policy and even the price of peanuts."
Hubert Green, the 1977 winner at Southern Hills

"In Europe this would not have happened . . . after this experience I may never come back to play in the US Open."
Seve after missing his tee time at Baltusrol in 1980 and being disqualified (In Europe they needed him more than he needed them!)

"Tough shit. That's been the rule for a hundred years."
JC Snead's reaction to Seve's trauma

"There's really not much to do. We're just mowing the greens and letting the rough grow. When it gets so that only a couple of guys on our staff can break 80 it will be ready."
Pebble Beach official on the 1982 Open preparations

"Watson is doing to Nicklaus what Nicklaus was doing to me 20 years ago. I knew exactly what Nicklaus was thinking when Watson's chip went in."
Palmer on Watson's Open winning shot at the 17th in 1982 (He wouldn't have been gloating, now would he?)

"That shot had more meaning to me than any other shot in my career."
Watson

"That took all the wind out of my sails and I just really never had a chance to get much going the rest of the year. It doesn't often happen with a shot by somebody else; you usually do it to yourself."
Nicklaus on the same incident

"There's going to be a lot of extra sales of Chapstick because the USGA officials are smiling so much."
Johnny Miller on the toughness of Pebble Beach in 1992

"The winds were howling, the greens were like linoleum floors, and the rough felt as if you were walking through a burial ground for sheepdogs."
Peter Jacobsen on the 1992 US Open at Pebble Beach

"The score is Tom Kite 1 US PGA 149. If they want greens like this, then I might as well take up topless darts."
Nick Faldo blaming the PGA for the sins of the USGA in 1992

"I've been over here since last Thursday, so I'm well prepared. If I don't win it this year, then perhaps next year I'll come over a month early and pitch up a tent on the first tee."
Faldo at Baltusrol in 1993. He didn't win.

THE OPEN CHAMPIONSHIP (THE BRITISH OPEN)

"It's almost like the eighth wonder of the world playing that tournament."
Lee Trevino

"I felt like a pimp being asked by the Pope to visit the Vatican."
The reaction of journalist Charles Price to a suggestion from Bobby Jones that he compete in the Open at St Andrews

"A rickety event in which Peter Thomson beat half a dozen guys from Stoke Poges."
Dan Jenkins on the Open before Palmer, Nicklaus and Player began to compete in it annually

"Any golfer worth his salt has to cross the sea and try to win the British Open."
Jack Nicklaus

"To me the Open is the tournament I would come to if I had to leave a month before and swim over."
Lee Trevino

"I've shrunk."
Gary Player – after being battered by wind and rain at the Open at Muirfield

"Suggest play off back tees for remainder of championship."
Caustic wire received by Muirfield Greens Committee after Hagen had shot a 67 in the 1929 Open

"Armour became the Open champion while working on his third highball."
Charles Price writing about the 1931 Open which Armour won an hour after the finish of his round

"What do I want with prestige? The British Open paid the winner $600 in American money. A man would have to be 200 years old at that rate to retire from golf."
Sam Snead explaining his reluctance to play in the Open after the war

"That ball was worth some cash, and Scotty proved it. An hour later he sold it for 50 quid. So he made more off the Open than I did."
Snead after giving his ball to his caddy in 1946. Scotty had told him tearfully, "I'll treasure it all my days."

"We were brought up thinking the British Open wasn't much of a deal, because they seemed so easy to beat."
Jackie Burke in the 1940s

"They couldn't have done it for a nicer fellow."
Bobby Locke on the suggestion that the nightly watering of the greens in Troon in 1950 put him at a distinct advantage

"I'll be back!"
Ben Hogan after winning at Carnoustie in 1953, on the only occasion he played in the British Open

"For years I came over trying hard to win. This year, I simply came back to see my friends."
Roberto di Vicenzo after winning in 1967, at Hoylake

"I had to lean sideways to see the top of the flag."
Gary Player on the accuracy of his fairway wood shot to the 14th at Carnoustie in 1968. He got an eagle and won the Open championship.

"God, Jack, I never knew anyone could be so scared, so frightened."
Tony Jacklin to Jack Nicklaus after his 1969 win at Royal Lytham

"Sanders was as jumpy as a cat – there was nothing I could do about it."
George Buss, Doug Sanders's caddy in 1970 at St Andrews where Sanders missed a short putt on 18 and tied Nicklaus. He lost the play-off.

Jacklin: "Lee, we don't need any conversation today."
Trevino: "Tony, you don't have to talk. You just have to listen."
Jacklin to Trevino before the final round in 1972

"It's all yours, Tony."
Trevino to Jacklin on the 17th at Muirfield in 1972, just before he sank a chip for a miraculous 5. Jacklin, off the green in two, took 6.

"I thought I'd blown it at the 17th green when I drove into a trap. God is a Mexican."
Trevino on his Muirfield win in 1972

"When things have gone against me, I have always tried harder because I felt I would always come out better at the other end. But this situation broke my faith in that. I can't explain it any other way."
Tony Jacklin on the manner in which he lost the 1972 Open to Lee Trevino

"My time is come."
Tom Watson on winning the 1975 Open at Carnoustie

Watson: "This is what it's all about, isn't it?"
Nicklaus: "You bet it is."
An exchange between the two great champions during their 1977 head-to-head at Turnberry

"He did what? Come on, he must have missed out some holes."
Hale Irwin at Lytham in 1979 after hearing that Seve had shot a 65 to his 68 in cold, windy conditions

"I like Cowboy and Indian books. I read that night until I forgot about my problems and started worrying about the Indians."
Seve on the eve of his 1979 Open victory

"When Ballesteros triumphed at the British Open in 1979, for his first major win, he hit so few fairways off the tee that he was often mistaken for a gallery marshall."
Dan Jenkins

"That the winner, Severiano Ballesteros, chose not to use it (the course) but preferred his own, which mainly consisted of hay fields, car parks, grand stands, dropping zones and even ladies' clothing, was his affair. Nevertheless he was a very worthy Open Champion."
Colin MacLaine, Chairman of the R&A Championship committee, on Seve's 1979 Lytham success

"If Nicklaus had been in some of the places I was at Lytham he'd have shot an 80."
Seve

"I'm just trying to finish, pal!"
Bill Rodgers, winner in 1981, to the policeman who tried to stop him getting to the final green

"I didn't win this championship, I had it given to me."
Tom Watson after the collapse of Nick Price and Bobby Clampett gifted him the 1982 Open at Troon

"I had my second place speech all prepared."
Tom Watson in 1982

"Maybe I should go to a sports shop and buy a trophy. That's the only way I'm going to get one."
Seve before the 1984 Open at St Andrews, which he duly won

"I've day-dreamed for years when I was a kid, of standing over a putt like that and saying to myself 'This to win the Open', and suddenly there is was."
Faldo after his 1987 win at Muirfield, his first major victory

"I don't think Daniel Boone could play it from there."
Seve declaring a shot unplayable at Royal Lytham in his Open victory of 1988

"I don't want to count myself out this year, but heck, I'd come back as a caddy."
Jack Nicklaus in 1991 talking about the Open, not reincarnation

"In the first month or so after winning the Open I seemed to be on the phone for six hours each day. The Claret Jug was always nearby and it became clear to Hayley that it was getting more attention from Daddy than she was. So I had to be careful that she didn't throw it on the fire."
Ian Baker-Finch, 1991 Open winner at Royal Birkdale

Reporter: "What do you think will be the key to winning here this week?"
Seve: "To see the ball after hitting it from the tee."
Seve at Muirfield in 1992

"If we open the course for one player we've got to open it for everyone. Mr Watson will be most welcome after the qualifying is over."
Secretary of North Berwick after throwing Tom Watson off the course between qualifying rounds for the 1992 Open

"This was one of those rare occasions when golf managed to get the dramatic balance right, leaving the stars to play their allotted roles and confining the light relief to the supporting players."
Peter Dobereiner on the 1993 Open at Royal St Georges, Sandwich, won by Greg Norman

US PGA CHAMPIONSHIP

"I don't think a tournament with such a long history and tradition of its own wants to be thought of as 'US Open: The Sequel'."
Peter Jacobsen

"Another weekend with nothing to do."
Arnold Palmer on missing the cut at the PGA

"It's perceived as a US Open-wannabe. The PGA sets up golf courses just as the Open does, with baked-out greens and pet cemetery rough."
Peter Jacobsen

"He may have gone to bed three hours ago. But he knows who he is playing. You can rest assured that he hasn't slept a wink."
Walter Hagen on an opponent when the PGA was a matchplay event

"The crowd was mumbling about Nicklaus, but I didn't need them to tell me that the Bear was coming."
Hal Sutton, who held off Nicklaus and won in 1983

"What do you guys want? You guys are never satisfied. Face it, you know I did a hell of a job today. Bob Tway just won the golf tournament."

Greg Norman's reaction in the press tent to Tway's outrageous chip-in on the 18th at Bellerive in 1986 to snatch the title

"Norman stood in the fringe and looked on incredulously. The two words he uttered were the same two that are heard on flight recorders retrieved from plane wreckage. The printable version is "Oh, no.""

Larry Dorman writing about the 1986 PGA

"Call it the Perspiring Golfers of America Championship . . . it might be easier to complete a triathlon than 72 holes on this swamp monster. The Bermuda rough is said to be deadlier than the Bermuda Triangle."

Tim Rosaforte's description of the 1987 event at Palm Beach when the temperature soared

"You're reduced to a hundred-yard swing with your buttocks clamped at 2,500 psi, hoping that the recipient of the venomous swipe doesn't fly out like a wounded snipe across the green straight into the very same crap."

David Feherty on the roughs at the 1992 PGA at Bellerive

"It feels like I finally got a monkey off my back – a whole troupe of them."

Nick Price after winning 1992 PGA at Bellerive, his first Major

"I'm not going to cry over this. These things happen. I can handle adversity pretty good."

Greg Norman on losing yet another Major, the 1993 PGA to Paul Azinger (Norman completed a reverse Grand Slam in the process, losing all four Majors in play-offs)

Fifth Hole: Amen Corner Par 4

Hole: 5th Royal Dublin
Par 4 465 yds
Designer: ES Colt

Tony Lema is alleged to have christened those three sphincter-tightening Augusta holes (11th 12th and 13th) "Amen Corner". Roughly translated "Amen" means "so be it", which makes this corner of a Georgia field sound forever tranquil. To the uninitiated there is more than a mere suggestion of resignation, of stoic acceptance – "I've just taken a quadruple bogey at the 12th . . . so be it!" Not so! Dump a ball into Rae's Creek and the overwhelming emotion is the desire to fill it in with quick-setting concrete.

Few get to experience that particular destructive and environmentally incorrect feeling because Augusta is relatively uncontaminated by golfers for most of the year. But we all have our Amen Corners and our Rae's Creeks. Yours may feature a 200-yard carry into the wind over rocks, water, alligators, coral and densely packed sargassum to a green twenty feet in circumference atop a 400-foot-high chalk cliff which can only be reached by a 1-iron shot off a downhill lie or it may be just a wispy privet hedge on a straightforward par 3 which acts as a powerful magnet for balata. Or both! Probably both!

Don't despair. Think of how Hitler felt after Stalingrad. Is four putting really worse? Would you prefer to play your approach from the car park or have had command of the Titanic as it ploughed into a casual iceberg? Let's face it, Julius Caesar had far more problems with the 15th than you'll ever have!

Frustration is to golf what disappointment is to the Lotto. It's what we've come to expect of the game. Even the greats are susceptible. Ben Crenshaw is not known as "Gentle Ben" for nothing. But nobody put a gun to his head and threatened to shoot him unless he smashed his putter during his Ryder Cup match in 1987 with Eamon Darcy. He did it of his own free temper. Corey Pavin didn't stop abusing his clubs until one day he took a swing at his bag with an iron and shattered his driver AND his putter.

Be philosophical! Do what all underachievers do at one time or another, look around for someone worse than yourself. Get their phone number. Invite them to play . . . regularly. In no time at all you'll begin to feel like a golfer. Then, with your confidence built up you can safely dump them and look around for someone a little better.

And remember, even for those scratch golfers whose game you overtly admire but covertly loathe, disaster lies just around the corner. Ask Tommy Armour. (Assuming you know an accommodating medium!) One week he wins the US Open, the next he takes a 21 on the 17th in the Shawnee Open. Life's a triple bogey!

HAZARDS AND HORRORS

"A ball will always travel farthest when hit in the wrong direction."
Henry Beard in "Mulligan's Laws"

"You can hit a 200-acre fairway 10% of the time and a two-inch branch 90% of the time."
Henry Beard in "Mulligan's Laws"

"What other four hours' activity can chasten a magnate with so rich a variety of disappointments, or unman a Lothario with so many rebuffed desires?"
John Updike

"Water holes are sacrificial waters where you make a steady gift of your pride and high-priced balls."
Tommy Bolt

"The number one thing when in trouble is: Don't get into more trouble."
Dave Stockton

"I was afraid to move my lips in front of TV. The Commissioner probably would have fined me just for what I was thinking."
Tom Weiskopf after taking a 13 in the 1980 Masters

"Shouldn't that dog have a cask around its neck?"
Unidentified journalist watching Arnold Palmer on the beach at Pebble Beach, failing to get the ball to the 17th green while watched by a lone dog

"I'm just having a bad day."
Frenchman Martin Goldberg to the official who asked him to withdraw from the Open pre-qualifying because he was 10 over after six holes

"Just remember it takes just as long to play your way out of a slump as it did to play your way into one."
The not-very-encouraging advice of Harvey Penick to his pupil Ben Crenshaw

"Has anyone got a Hamlet?"
David Feherty recalling the famous cigar ad as he walked off the 13th at Fulford after taking an 11

"Mr RJ Barton was approaching the green of a blind hole 354 yards long, when his ball struck a caddy, named John McNiven, on the head as he was replacing the flag in the hole. The ball rebounded 42 yards 2 feet 10 inches, which distance was measured twice in the presence of three people."
"The Golfer's Handbook" – we don't discover the fate of the caddy

"The difference between a sand trap and water is the difference between a car crash and an aeroplane crash. You have a chance of recovering from a car crash."
Bobby Jones

"No, go right ahead, hook some more."
Trevino wryly talking to a ball bound for perdition

"That the water in the bunker at the 13th be changed."
A "suggestion" from Lord Brabazon. It was his way of complaining that Royal St Georges, Sandwich, was waterlogged.

"In the United States competitions with nondescript hazards, such as suspended barrels to be played through and gates to be played around, are frequently held to provide what are supposed to be amusing variations of the game."
"The Golfer's Handbook" (sniffing disapprovingly)

"After that, I got myself together and bogeyed the last three."
Ben Crenshaw after an 11

"Why do people panic in bunkers? First of all, a bunker is defined as a hazard by rules, and anything that's called a hazard must be hazardous, right?"
Nancy Lopez

"At Rose Bay, New South Wales, DJ Bayly MacArthur, on steppng into a bunker, began to sink. He shrieked for help and was rescued when up to his armpits."
"The Golfer's Handbook"

"I used a tree iron."
Bernhard Langer on his club selection from a shot from a tree at Fulford in 1981

"Because I had a long putt for an 11."
Clayton Heafner on being asked why he had taken a 12 on one hole

"I expected to be playing my third drive here on Saturday afternoon, not Thursday morning."
Peter Jacobsen after losing two balls off a tee at Royal St Georges in 1985

"He played almost the entire final round without putting his spikes on the fairway. He spent so much time in the sand that if you held his wedge to your ear, you could hear the ocean."
Joe Gergen on JC Snead's awful round at the 1978 US Open at Cherry Hills

"It was just my luck to score a hole in one when I didn't want to."
Mark Law, from Oxfordshire, who was actually competing in a long driving competition when he accomplished his ace

"If golf has a defect, it is that it prevents a man being a whole-hearted lover of nature. Where the layman sees waving grass and romantic tangles of undergrowth your golfer beholds nothing but a nasty patch of rough from which he must divert his ball."

PG Wodehouse

"My mother told me there would be days like these."

Jeff Sluman after losing the 1992 World Matchplay final 8 & 7 to Nick Faldo

"It was a horrendous week for me because I played so bad. I couldn't hit a cow's backside with a banjo."

David Llewellyn on the Welsh World Cup win in 1987 which he attributed entirely to the play of his teammate Ian Woosnam

"Well I guess your small British ball helped me some. If I'd had to play the big ball, I'd have been all over the place."

Walter Danecki from Milwaukee after recording rounds of 108 and 113 (81 over par) in the 1965 British Open qualifier

"It was the first thing I had hit all day."

The candid admission of 69-year-old Derek Gatley when he came to, after hitting himself on the head with his own golf club (the shaft broke)

"I tried to make a one, but I made two of them instead."

US Senior, Al Kelley, talking after making an 11

"Oh I'm much worse, old boy – I'm a carrier."

A shanking victim talking to fellow shanker Henry Longhurst

"I can't believe this has happened to me. I thought I was in a war-zone. I didn't know much about the first strike but two of the lads were helping me to my feet when there was a shout of 'Fore'. They hit the deck, left me staggering about and the ball whacked me in the middle of the back. I stumbled, went down again and just flaked out. Now they want me to hold the flag on every hole so they can be sure of hitting the target."

Surrey pub landlord, Jim Meade, who has the unique distinction of being hit twice within a minute by flying golf balls

TEMPER, TEMPER

"You'd better throw a provisional, that one's likely to be lost."
Playing partner to Tommy Bolt after he threw a club into a lake

"Of all the games man has devised, supposedly for his enjoyment, golf is in a class by itself in the anguish it inflicts."
Herbert Warren Wind

"When I played, I never lost my temper. Sometimes, it is true, I may, after missing a shot, have broken my club across my knees; but I did it in a calm and judicial spirit, because the club was obviously no good and I was going to get another one anyway."
"The Oldest Member" in PG Wodehouse's "Ordeal by Golf"

"Good golfing temperament falls between taking it with a grin or shrug and throwing a fit."
Sam Snead

"Sometimes you'd like to just stand there in the middle of the green and scream as loud as you can. But we're the perfect gentlemen."
Raymond Floyd

"Armando was round in 76, but more importantly his putter was still in one piece. The day before, after missing a short putt on the 6th green, he dealt himself a blow on the forehead and the shaft snapped. He used his 3-iron and two paracetamol for the remaining 12 holes and scored level par."
Mark Roe on Armando Saavedra

"You son of a bitch!"
Curtis Strange to an annoying photographer during the 1989 PGA Championship

"What would Mr Jones think?"
The father of Jack Nicklaus invoking the name of the great Bobby Jones whenever young Jack lost his temper on the course

"He once played the front nine with a new set (of clubs) and, at the turn, junked them and bought another new one for the back nine."
Jim Murray on Mickey Rooney's club-throwing habits

"Knowingly killing a goose out of season and being illegally in possession of a dead Canada goose."
Charges laid against a Canadian doctor who killed a goose with his putter after it hissed at the wrong time

"Why do I play this ****** game? I do hate it so."
The writer Bernard Darwin, overheard in the rough

"One of these days I'm going to put on a club-throwing contest to show you boys just how stupid you really look."
Harry Stephens, pro at Druid Hills in Atlanta (He did, the winning throw was 61 yards)

"You little ****** ! Never presume upon my good nature again!"
Unidentitifed Scot hurling his putter against a stone wall near the 9th in Muirfield

"A cardinal rule for the club-breaker is never to break your putter and driver in the same match or you are dead."
Tommy "Thunder" Bolt

Caddy: "Mr Bolt, you'll be using either a 2 or a 3-iron for this shot."
Bolt: "Hell man, that's 350 yards out there. Ol' Tom can't begin to reach the green with a 2, much less a 3-iron."
Caddy: "Mr Bolt, all you got left in your bag are those two clubs, unless you want to use your putter, and that's missing its handle, you snapped it off on the first nine."
A reported exchange between "Thunder" Bolt and his caddy

"Actually, I was always more of a breaker than a thrower – most of them putters. I broke so many of those, I probably became the world's foremost authority on how to putt without a putter."
Tommy Bolt

"If you're going to throw a club in temper, it's important to throw it ahead of you in the direction of the green. That way you don't waste energy going back to pick it up."
Tommy Bolt

"Why, during those early days Palmer was on tour, he threw them. I have to say that he was the very worst golf-club thrower I have ever seen. He had to learn to play well, he'd never have made it as a thrower."

Tommy Bolt on Arnold Palmer

"The most exquisitely satisfying act in the world of golf is that of throwing a club. The full backswing, the delayed wrist action, the flowing follow-through, followed by that unique whirring sound, reminiscent only of a passing flock of starlings, are without parallel in sport."

Henry Longhurst

"Never talk to my golf ball, goddammit, never talk to my golf ball."

Peter Teravainen finding an unlikely way of taking it out on his caddy

"I've got this new driver, persimmon head, graphite shaft, 12 degree loft. It goes ten yards further than any club I've ever thrown."

Comedian Tom O'Connor quoting English pro Alan Egford

BAD BOYS

"Professional golf has become a game with too much character and not enough characters."

Thomas Boswell

"The departure of Dean Martin from a golf club is comparable to a nearsighted millionaire leaving a crap game in a smoky room."

Jim Murray, US journalist

"He knows how to live. The breweries will have to go on overtime while he is in the money, and everybody had better lock up their daughters."

Peter Dobereiner on Trevino

"People say it was amazing that Jimmy could win three Masters almost without practising. I think it's amazing he could win them almost without sleeping."

Sam Snead on Jimmy Demaret

"In a golf club everyone knows the player who does not replace his divot. One can guess how he leads the rest of his life."

Shivas Irons, mythical Scottish pro in Michael Murphy's novel "Golf in the Kingdom"

"Tommy Bolt's putter has spent more time in the air than Lindbergh."

Jimmy Demaret

"I've thrown or broken a few clubs in my day. In fact, I guess at one time or another I probably held distance records for every club in the bag."

Tommy Bolt

"An unplayable lie."

Bobby Locke's description of a fellow professional's wife

"I guess my game isn't built around an early morning start."

Doug Sanders after putting his approach to the 1st at St Andrews into the Swilcan Burn in 1970

"In the US Open in San Francisco, I walked into the locker room and there were 25 guys and I didn't know one of them. I said, 'Can I bum a cigarette off somebody?' and they all looked at each other like I was crazy. So I went to Nicky Price's locker, got a cigarette out, lit it and all 25 guys got up and left."

Lee Trevino

"He had the flashiest clothes and the flashiest women . . . I spent a night in his place in Dallas once. All he had in it was booze and about 150 pairs of golf shoes."

Lee Trevino on Doug Sanders

"Brother, the provocation was ample."

A Northampton vicar to his playing partner after the latter had dumped a ball into a bunker and uttered unrepeatable profanities

"His obligation to go out to parties was reinforcd by his love of parties. Naturally his golf suffered but that was just one of the hazards of being Christy O'Connor."

Peter Dobereiner on "Himself"

"He looks for them in the gallery, and man, he spots one, we gotta lose three strokes."

Doug Sanders's caddie on his boss's search for the perfect woman

"Raymond [Floyd] has done it all. If he were playing Sunday in Miami and there was a party that night in Dallas, he'd charter a plane."

Lanny Wadkins on Floyd, the party animal

"Hell, I don't even get up at that hour to close the window."

Walter Hagen declining an early tee time

"I've an idea he's broken eleven of the Ten Commandments, but I'll tell you something else, Father, I think I'd like to be with Hagen wherever he goes when he dies."

Fred Corcoran, golf entrepreneur and manager to a priest, about Walter Hagen

"The record books have me down for a 79 on the final day. That looks pretty woeful, but considering what happened the night before it was a pretty good round of golf."

"Champagne" Tony Lema talking about the 1959 San Diego Open

"I've been known to party day and night. Heck, in Las Vegas I paid a guy $50 an hour to sleep for me."

Doug Sanders

"I can't believe the actions of some of our top pros. They should have side jobs modelling for Pampers."

Fuzzy Zoeller

"I'm not asleep, just resting my eyes."

Christy O'Connor Sr denying to Dai Rees that he had fallen asleep while standing up at a hotel reception desk

"If profanity had an influence on the flight of the ball, the game would be played far better than it is."

Horace Hutchinson

"I regret it all happened at the US Open. I regret missing the experience of completing the second round. I should have known not to start it. I lacked experience, but do people really think I did it on purpose to annoy anyone?"

Rafferty after walking off the course at the US Open

"In hockey a gang rape accusation will get you traded. Unless you're a 40 goal-scorer. Then you can stay. In boxing, if you've been convicted of murder, don't hide it. Put it in your promoter's résumé, then recite your cellblock number by heart. In golf, however, everybody is perfect. How lucky for golf. How unlucky for John Daly."

Thomas Boswell on golf's latest "bad boy"

"That's the most expensive bowl of pasta I've ever had."

Mark Roe after being fined £100 for a food fight with Russell Claydon

GROUCHES

Jenkins: "Tam Arte Quam Marte. What does that mean?"
Kimball: "Eat Shit and Die."

George Kimball, with his own translation of the Troon motto after a bad day, to Dan Jenkins

"Seve Ballesteros poured so much oil on troubled waters yesterday that he was in danger of creating an environmental disaster to rival the Exxon Valdez."

Dermot Gilleece of the Irish Times *on Seve's press conference after the Ryder Cup venue for 1997 had been annouced*

Snead: "If I putted like Jack Nicklaus, I'd have won a thousand tournaments."
Bolt: "If Jack played in as many tournaments as you, he'd have won two thousand."

Sam Snead and Tommy Bolt

"He runs and lifts weights and eats health foods. That's all well and good, but I get tired of hearing him brag about it. So what if he has the most perfect bowel movements on the tour."

Dave Hill on Gary Player

"Doug Sanders has said he likes to have sex and a hot-tub bath every morning and he's loose and ready to go. Of course, if Sanders had scored half as often with women as he claims he has, he'd be dead."
Dave Hill

"The hero-worshippers in his gallery ought to appreciate that somebody has to play along with Arnold to keep his score, if nothing else."
Dave Hill

"I only came here because I heard the Irish hate the British as much as I do."
Dave Hill visiting Dublin

"In my time in the States I found a lot of small-minded guys – and I'm afraid Dave Hill was one of them – who didn't like foreigners on their tour."
Tony Jacklin

"I wish to goodness I knew the man who invented this infernal game. I'd strangle him. But I suppose he's been dead for ages. Still, I could go and jump on his grave."
"Ferdinand Dibble" in PG Wodehouse's "The Heart of a Goof"

"You can win this. You should. But you won't. Because you play 'jolly golf'."
Ben Hogan to Claude Harmon about the US Open at Winged Foot in 1959

"I played crap, he played crap. He just out-crapped me."
Wayne Grady after losing in the 1990 World Matchplay to Greg Norman at the 38th

"It's like replacing Bo Derek with Roseanne Barr."
Johnny Miller on replacing Cypress Point with Poppy Hills for the AT&T Pro-Am (The remark cost him a $1,000 fine)

"I didn't like the food over there."
Sam Snead on why he didn't defend his 1946 Open title

"I guess I had something else to do."
Ben Hogan on why he didn't defend his 1953 Open title

"I know where all the holes are. Unlike the USGA, the R&A doesn't get some turkeys to go and change the holes around."
Lanny Wadkins explaining why he wasn't playing a practice round at St Andrews before the Open

"I'm surprised he didn't drown, because he can't keep his mouth shut."
Nicklaus's reaction to Jerry Pate diving into a pond on winning a tournament

"He has two moods 1) annoyed 2) about to be annoyed."
Journalist Rick Reilly writing about Nick Faldo in Sports Illustrated

"He's crazy. He needs to start wearing a hat. I think the sun has baked his brain."
Reilly on Faldo's rejection of quotes Reilly attributed to him

"I told them, 'If you want to laugh, you have two choices, either go to a circus or I'll bury this 8-iron in your head.'"
David Graham to fans at the British Open in 1981

Sixth Hole: Star Wars Par 3

Hole: 6th Killarney (Killeen)
Par 3 195 yds
Designer: Dr Billy O'Sullivan/Eddie Hackett

Maurice G Flitcroft is a star in his own right and a thoroughgoing golf fan, a hardnecked enthusiast not content to bide his time on the far side of the ropes watching his heroes shoot the lights out of golf courses up and down the country. Like all the rest of us he wants to be out there with them, to be a fan with a caddy. Unlike the rest of us he has gone to extraordinary lengths to do something about it.

His activities have drawn blood from the Royal and Ancient, R&A Secretary Michael Bonallack describes him as "nothing more than an irritation and a nuisance." Granted, that is a valid point of view. Maurice G Flitcroft is indeed an irritation and a nuisance, but he is also Everygolfer, the Pro within us all.

He first came to public attention when he shattered the world record for an Open prequalifying event at Formby near Liverpool, taking 121 shots to go around the course. His achievement was all the more monumental when you consider that it was his first time on a golf course, and he was not, as he had represented himself to the organisers, a member of the PGA. The PGA's loss I say!

That was the last time he entered the Open under his own name. In 1978 he became Gene Pacecki, an American pro trying to make it to St Andrews. After taking 70 by the time he reached the 10th green he pulled out of the tournament before irate R&A officials (who, by now, had recognised him) moved in. Two years later a Swiss professional, under the name of Gerald Hoppy, attempted to prequalify and take his place among the greats at Muirfield. He got as far as the 9th before his ball was lifted by two outside agencies. He was escorted from the precincts and banished into the outer darkness.

During the 1990 Open qualifier at Ormskirk another American

competitor, the little-known James Beau Jolley, got as far as the 3rd before being unmasked. Given his age (64) how long will it be before Maurice realises that his true destiny lies on the Seniors tour in the USA where personality, character and bizarre golf swings are nurtured and appreciated. When that realisation finally dawns the Michael Bonallacks of this world will waken up to the fact that the great original, whose development they have stifled, has abandoned them to their rules and idiotic conventions and gone to a place where his genius is appreciated.

THE RYDER CUP

"My heartfelt best wishes are extended to Valderrama and Mr Patino . . . I wanted Novo Sancti Petri, but sometimes life is not so sweet. We do not always get what we want."
Seve after Valderrama was chosen as the Spanish venue for the 1997 Ryder Cup. Ballesteros had earlier accused the Valderrama course of offering him a one million bribe to push its cause.

"I think Mr Patino should be the captain."
Seve joking about the Valderrama owner, when asked who should captain the 1997 European team

"The Ryder Cup, the biennial match-play competition in which top American professionals play top European professionals for a jug."
Michael Bamberger

"Jerry had everything – from the neck down. With my brains and his swing, we were unbeatable."
Lee Trevino on his Ryder Cup partner Jerry Pate

"We had six players in our team worth their salt, but the other six were only putting the blazer on."
Brian Huggett, former Captain, on some of the British and Irish Ryder Cup teams

"They should have been telling our players, 'Let's go out and win,' rather than what became the catch phrase, 'Let's go out and put up a good show.'"
Christy O'Connor Sr on British and Irish Ryder cup captains during his record ten appearances

"It is humiliating to have someone steal your game and then beat you at it in 23 of the 30 Ryder Cup matches ever played. In the British eye, that is a public hanging. To the British ego, it is twenty lashes at the mast."

American journalist Clayton Hoskins

"I didn't think anything could be worse than the final hole of a Major, when you are trying to protect the lead, but today I felt twice as bad as I've ever felt. I couldn't eat."

Paul Azinger on playing in the Ryder Cup

"I know what it means to have your brains beaten out. I know what it feels like to sit at the back of the aeroplane and wear plastic shoes. It just makes you feel embarrassed."

Tony Jacklin on the second class treatment of some of the Ryder Cup teams he played for

"It's hard to figure out. They're the greatest players in the world."

Roger Maltbie being sarcastic at the height of 1980s European domination of the Ryder Cup, when asked why no European had won the US Open since 1970

"It has gone past being a match. It has become life and death."

Nick Faldo

"If a guy says it's against his religion tell him to get another religion."

Lanny Wadkins on practice round betting during the Ryder Cup

"This is not for money – we play here, from the heart."

Seve Ballesteros

"Let us hope our team will win, but it is the play without the Prince of Denmark."

Samuel Ryder to Abe Mitchell in 1927 after the latter was forced to withdraw from the first Ryder Cup match

Palmer: "Good morning, Captain."
Hogan: "Good morning, Arnold, you're a day late."
Palmer: "I've been in England winning the World Matchplay Championship. (Pause) What ball are we playing?"
Hogan: "Who said you are playing, Arnold?"

1967 US Ryder Cup team Captain Ben Hogan showing who's boss

"Ladies and Gentlemen, the United States Ryder Cup team – the finest golfers in the world."
Hogan introducing the members of the US team in 1967 (Britain and Ireland lost by an embarrassing 15 point margin)

"They asked me if I'd like to go and attend the matches as an official. I told them to stick it in their ear."
Jacklin after being dropped from the 1981 Ryder Cup (The Europeans lost)

"When I played Ryder Cup foursomes with him, I could hit the ball anywhere and he would still manage to put the ball on the green."
Paul Way on playing with Seve in 1983

"When Jack Nicklaus told me I was playing Ballesteros I took so many pills that I'm glad they don't have drug tests for golfers."
Fuzzy Zoeller in 1983 (Europe lost by a point)

"I wish I was playing in the Ryder Cup. How could they beat me? I've been struck by lightning, had two back operations and been divorced twice."
Lee Trevino in 1985 (Maybe the Americans could have done with him, they lost)

"You'd have thought they'd introduced us not as America's Best Golfers but as America's Most Wanted."
Peter Jacobsen on the muted reaction to the introduction of himself and playing partner Curtis Strange at the Belfry in 1985 for a foursomes match with Ian Woosnam and Paul Way

"Ryder Cup golf is all about hard work. There are no shortcuts, nowhere to hide – ever."
Ian Woosnam in 1987

"I'm trying to convince myself I'm happy."
Seve before the 1987 Ryder Cup at Muirfield Village

"I'm very happy."
Seve after the European win

"I'd be lying if I said I wasn't nervous. But I wasn't shaking enough to miss the putt."

Eamon Darcy after sinking the putt that beat Ben Crenshaw and won the Cup

"The moment which I will always remember from Muirfield Village was when Eamon Darcy holed that downhill putt on the final green to win his singles match against Ben Crenshaw. I still can't get that putt out of my mind."

Ryder Cup captain in 1987, Tony Jacklin

"If there is any crowd problem, any real sign of hooliganism, then I have a simple solution to it – end the Ryder Cup. Right there, right then, we should scrap it. This is a game of golf, not a war."

Tony Jacklin before the Belfry meeting in 1989, another European victory

"I lost for twelve guys and their wives and the Captain. I was a mess, I didn't leave the locker room for two hours."

Fred Couples after losing to Christy O'Connor Jr in their singles at the Belfry in 1989

"Just hold on, honey!"

Ben Crenshaw to his heavily pregnant wife in 1989

"I remember looking at Seve and thinking he looked smaller. He wasn't smaller, but I just felt bigger. It's a case of growing into the job."

David Feherty after playing in his first Ryder Cup match at Kiawah Island in 1991

"If I make the team it will be incredible. In other years when Swedes have been doing well everyone starts talking about it, and they start playing badly."

Sweden's Per Ulrik Johannson in 1991 (He didn't make the team)

"Playing against Lanny is like having a bulldog tied to your ankle."

1991 US Captain Dave Stockton on Lanny Wadkins

"The golf course is so hard it's unbelievable. Nick [Faldo] and I have just said we don't know if we could have finished if we'd had a card in our hands."
Raymond Floyd on the Ocean Course at Kiawah Island

"I've had a bad week. But in the real world a bad week is waking up and finding you're a steelworker in Scunthorpe."
Faldo in 1991

"It would have been quite easy to have blamed God and say 'Why me?' I felt God wanted to test my faith, to see if I really loved him. I look at it this way. There has only been one perfect man in this world and we crucified him. All I did was miss a putt."
Bernhard Langer on the infamous missed putt at the 18th at Kiawah Island in 1991. He halved his match with Hale Irwin but Europe lost the Cup.

"Should the rest of us change?"
Sam Torrance after Seve Ballesteros turned up for a 1993 Ryder Cup team photo in the wrong jumper

"To sit and watch all day was very hard. I generated enough stomach acid to take the chrome off my irons."
Lanny Wadkins on sitting out the final day of the 1993 Ryder Cup

"It was a great day for golf. The competition was so intense you could have written a novel about it."
1993 US Captain Tom Watson on the narrow American win

"I would see a match at Valderrama being like the Americans playing at home."
Seve Ballesteros launching the bid of (Seve-designed) Novo Sancti Petri for the 1997 Ryder Cup

RIVALRIES

"A golf match is a test of your skill against your opponent's luck."
Henry Beard in "Mulligan's Laws"

"Secret disbelief in the enemy's play is useful."
Sir Walter Simpson on "The Art of Golf"

"It can truthfully be stated, I think, that outscoring his opponent does wonders for a golfer's morale, but what really sets him up on a cloud is outscoring himself."
Herbert Warren Wind

"I wouldn't hurt a chicken crossing the road, but if I got a man in trouble on the golf course, I'd kick the hell out of him. I don't care if he's my best friend."
Sam Snead

"I really don't like play-offs. I feel sorry for the other guy if I win and I feel worse if I lose."
Chi Chi Rodriguez

"The sport isn't like any other where a player can take out all that is eating him on an opponent. In golf, it's strictly you against your clubs."
Bob Rosburg, player and commentator

"A liar and a thief."
Mac O'Grady on his long-time adversary, US PGA Tour Commissioner Deane Beman (O'Grady also, inter alia, compared Beman to Adolf Hitler)

"We have a very old saying back in Ireland, 'The last shall be first'."
Harry Bradshaw to a Canada Cup (now World Cup) official after arriving in Mexico with Christy O'Connor a day late in 1958. The Irish team won.

"If we can't beat Paraguay then we might as well all go home."
Colin Montgomerie before Scotland were beaten 2-1 by Paraguay in the 1993 Dunhill Cup

"They will never believe this result back home."
Raul Fretes after beating "Monty" to win the tie

"We got whipped. Let's get the hell out of here."
Tom Kite after the USA lost to France in the first round of the 1990 Dunhill Cup

"I play with friends, but we don't play friendly games."
Ben Hogan

"Everyone's out there whoopin' and hallerin' for that son of a bitch, when they should be cheerin' ol' Tom."
Tommy Bolt on Arnold Palmer

"They ranged across golf courses like a team of Irish setters, concerned to cover the maximum ground with the minimum of restraint. They were an attractively volatile and mercurial bunch."
"Laddie" Lucas on Irish amateur golf teams of the 1930s

THE FAN

"The odds of hitting a duffed shot increase by the square of the number of people watching."
Henry Beard in "Mulligan's Laws"

"Rule One: Whenever a spectator seeks out a really good vantage point and settles down on shooting stick or canvas chair, the tallest and fattest golf-watcher on the course will take up station directly in front."
Peter Dobereiner

"I like golf because when somebody tells the gallery to be quiet, they get quiet. Try that in baseball and they get louder."
Mark McGuire, baseball first baseman

"A woman had me autograph a five dollar bill once and told me she would keep it for the rest of her life. A half hour later, I bought some drinks with a twenty. The change came back and the five was in it."
Lee Trevino

"Top Ten Reasons why we're Mochrie's Maniacs.
10. We heard there was free beer.
9. Our lives are empty and meaningless anyways, so what do we have to lose?
8. Dottie promised us a Rolex.
7. It sounds better than "Burton's Buddies."

6. It beats sitting at home watching reruns of *The Munsters*.
5. Our AA counsellor said we needed an extra-curricular activity.
4. We thought the shirts were witty.
3. The Judge ordered us to perform 50 hours of community service and this is all we could think of.
2. We like women with lots of earrings.
   . . . and the #1 reason why we're Mochrie's Maniacs:
1. Patty Sheehan wouldn't return our calls."
   T-shirt text worn by Chris Killer, LPGA Tour player Dottie Mochrie's biggest fan

"There is one statistical category on the tour in which I will always be number one, and that is Leading Tacklers. I have one, and everybody else is tied for second with none."
   Peter Jacobsen, who took on and brought down a streaker during the 1985 British Open

"I don't like it when people cheer me. I like it better when they cheer against me."
   Seve Ballesteros

"I have no patience with the golf pests who slap you on the back and ask you if you don't remember how they bought you a Moxie at Worcester in '25, or the time they acted as marshal at an exhibition in '27 at the Old Rough and Ready Country Club. I can't help being short with those intruders."
   Gene Sarazen

"If they could abstain from talking while you are playing, and if the shadow of their dresses would not flicker on the putting green while you are holing out, other objections might perhaps be waived."
   Lord Moncrieff of Tulliebole on women spectators

"Don't worry folks, it's only my career."
   Fuzzy Zoeller to two spectators laughing at his play

"Guarantee me three million a year and you can scream, yell, or spit on my ball when I'm putting. Because even if I miss I still get paid."
   Lee Trevino on fans who think a golf tournament should be like a baseball game

"The normal routine at Carroll's Irish Opens is for the fans to stroll outside the fairway ropes watching a favourite player until a leaderboard gives news of exciting deeds elsewhere. Then like a herd of wildebeeste catching the scent of a lion, they wheel and stampede across the course, pushing and jostling, invariably with men in holy orders producing unholy disorder as they elbow their way to the front with never so much as a Nunc Dimittis."
Peter Dobereiner

"If Arnold asked all of those people to go jump into the river for him, they would march straight to the river and jump."
Gary Player talking about "Arnie's Army", Arnold Palmer's supporters in the 1960s

"You're the man."
The modern catchcry of the demented and unimaginative fan

"Opinions are like bums, everybody's got one."
Tony Jacklin

"Individually they are pretty nice folks. But get them together and they are about as miserable a bunch of people as you could ever have the misfortune to run into in a supposedly civilised world."
Tommy Bolt on British fans

"Rubbish, his tee never went backwards."
Spectator on first tee at Birkdale in 1976 after Jack Nicklaus had just powered a drive down the fairway

"A number of years ago it dawned on me that the biggest seller at golf tournaments were those periscopes."
PGA Tour commissioner Deane Beman on why he championed the idea of "Stadium" golf

"I thought they had plenty in their bags."
The lady who stole DJ Russell's ball on the 18th at the 1991 Cannes Open

"I drew a big gallery today, I was paired with Palmer."
Gene Littler, US pro

"All I could think of was those movies and what Texans did to strangers they didn't like. Nine out of ten they get lynched. I really was afraid I might get lynched."

Aussie, Bruce Crampton, after the 1957 Houston Open

Seventh Hole: In the Swing Par 5

Hole: 7th K Club
Par 5 608 yds
Designer: Arnold Palmer & Ed Seay

STONE DEAD – THE ART OF PUTTING
A long, well-paced, luxuriant stroke and the ball is propelled towards
the hole. It drops in, to eloquent applause from your peers. But then
potting the final black in the snooker room after your round is easy.
It's different out there on those greens. They're always too fast (or
too slow), undulating (or too flat), bone dry (or too well watered),
sparse (or too hairy). Haven't you noticed that when every other
aspect of your game is purring along like a Silver Ghost your putting
reminds you of an ATM which keeps flashing the message that there
is no money in your account. Even the mighty are thus afflicted.
Bernhard Langer is the best-known conqueror of the dreaded "yips",
(the equivalent of "writer's block" to the golfer). The great American,
Raymond Floyd, once left his putter in a restaurant with a note
attached which read, "If anyone decides to steal this putter, let
them." Peter Alliss became such an excellent TV commentator
because he gave up the game when he realised he couldn't sink a
glass-bottomed boat with a pick-axe. Included elsewhere in this
chapter are some of the more poignant jeremiads lamenting what
Bobby Jones called "a curious sort of game within a game."

THE SWING

"The less skilled the player the more likely he is to share his ideas
about the golf swing."
Henry Beard in "Mulligan's Laws"

"To get an elementary grasp of the game of golf, a human must learn, by endless practice, a continuous and subtle series of highly unnatural movements, involving about 64 muscles, that result in a seemingly 'natural' swing, taking all of two seconds to begin and end."

Alistair Cooke

"The game has its sensuous pleasures, when you make the perfect swing and execute the shot precisely as you had planned it."

Peter Alliss

"I remember being upset once and telling my Dad I wasn't following through right, and he replied, 'Nancy, it doesn't make any difference to a ball what you do after you hit it.'"

Nancy Lopez

"Miss 'em quick."

American writer MacDonald Smith

"Golf swings are like snowflakes, no two are exactly alike."

Peter Jacobsen

"Your weight should be evenly distributed and that often takes years because the average person with a fat stomach usually has narrow legs and the matter of transferring part of the tonnage from one side to another can only be accomplished by studying evenings."

Ring Lardner

"If a lot of people gripped a knife and fork like they do a golf club, they'd starve to death."

Sam Snead

"Try to show me a champion who doesn't move his head during his golf swing. You can't do it."

Harvey Penick

"I was so impressed that during the last round, when my swing started to leave me, I started imitating his. And it worked too. Fact is, I almost caught him with his own swing."

Walter Hagen on Harry Vardon's swing

"Anytime a golfer hits a ball perfectly straight with a big club it is, in my view, a fluke."
Jack Nicklaus

"You don't hit anything with your backswing. So don't rush it."
Doug Ford, pro

"Slow is fast, fast is short."
Don January

"Nobody ever swung the club too slowly."
Bobby Jones

"You've got to 'own' the club at the top. You can't 'own' it if you swing too fast."
Tommy Bolt

"Golferswhotalkfastswingfast."
Bob Toski

"Swing fast and you'll never last, but swing slow and you'll make the dough."
Gary Player

"American players look as if they have all been cast in one admirable mould. Ours look as if they came out of innumerable different ones, and as if in nearly every mould there had been some flaw."
Bernard Darwin, writing half a century ago

"Most of us cannot let go and let the genie out of the lamp. We know he's in there, hidden in our bones and muscles, because he does come out now and then. When he does we wind up asking him for ten more yards on the drives, and he goes back in."
John Updike

"When Miller swings it looks like his golf club gets caught in a clothesline."
Ben Crenshaw on Miller Barber's swing

"My swing is no uglier than Arnold Palmer's, and it's the same ugly swing every time."
  Nancy Lopez

"He looks like someone delivering a pizza."
  Commentator Ben Wright on American pro Duffy Waldorf's swing

"Aw, that's just Hubert Green over there fixing his golf swing."
  Fuzzy Zoeller on Hubert Green's swing – after a chainsaw started up near US Open practice tee

"I don't try to analyse my swing. I looked at it once on film and almost got sick."
  Hubert Green on his own swing

"Doug Sanders braces himself with a wide stance that looks like a sailor leaning into a northeast gale and takes the club back barely far enough to get it off the ground."
  The late Tony Lema on Sanders's inimitable swing

"The only thing you should force in a golf swing is the club back into the bag."
  Byron Nelson

"I can see you're a fisherman."
  Ray Floyd to Brian Barnes as he managed to stop halfway through his downswing after his ball toppled off its tee

"Take it easily and lazily, because the golf ball isn't going to run away from you while you're swinging."
  Sam Snead

"You show me a player who swings out of his shoes and I'll show you a player who isn't going to win enough to keep himself in a decent pair of shoes for very long."
  Sam Snead

"I still swing the way I used to, but when I look up the ball is going in a different direction."
  Lee Trevino

TEE TO GREEN

"A ball hit to the wrong green will always land two feet from the hole."
Henry Beard in "Mulligan's Laws"

"If there is a ball in the fringe and a ball in the bunker the ball in the bunker is yours."
Henry Beard in "Mulligan's Laws"

"If Jack Nicklaus had to play my tee shots he couldn't break 80. He'd be a pharmacist with a string of drug stores in Ohio."
Lee Trevino

"I know that's why we play golf, to hit the ball into the hole. But it's such a strange feeling when you hit a shot and it actually goes in."
American pro Hollis Stacy after holing a 7-iron from more than 120 yards at the 1984 US Women's Open

"Only God can save that one."
US amateur Matt Palacio watching his ball head towards the rocks on the 18th at Pebble Beach during the 1965 Crosby Pro-Am

"Thank you God!"
Matt Palacio watching his ball hit a rock and bounce back onto the fairway as the waves miraculously receded

"If I'da cleared the trees and drove the green, it woulda been a great tee shot."
Sam Snead

"There are no short hitters on tour anymore – just long and unbelievably long."
Sam Snead

"I'd much rather be hitting the driver and a 9-iron out of the rough than hitting a driver and a 4-iron out of the fairway."
Jack Nicklaus

"Anybody who's played as long as I have and hit the ball as I do has got to be tough. You've got to be thick-skinned when you're looking at the green with a 4-wood in your hand."
Deane Beman, US PGA Tour Commissioner, on his lack of distance off the tee

"Right string, wrong yo-yo."
Chi Chi Rodriguez watching a ball going through the back of the green

"The good chip is like the good sand trap shot, it's your secret weapon. It allows you to whistle while you walk in the dark alleys of golf."
Tommy Bolt

"I hit a 341-yard drive in Hawaii once. It was downhill, downwind, down everything."
Laura Davies

"I hate to hook. It nauseates me. I could vomit when I see one. It's like a rattlesnake in your pocket."
Ben Hogan

"If you think the game is just a matter of getting it close and letting the law of averages do your work for you, you'll find a different way to miss every time."
Jack Nicklaus

"I can airmail the golf ball, but sometimes I don't put the right address on it."
Jim Dent, noted for his big hitting

"Airmail without zip code will never find its target."
Bob Toski

"I'll take anything in the air that doesn't sting."
Dave Marr

"He could not play any course twice in the same day . . . he was so accurate, that in his second round his shots finished in the divot holes he had made in the morning."
Henry Cotton on Harry Vardon's much-vaunted accuracy

"As the club began to descend she perceived that she underestimated the total of her errors. And when the ball, badly topped, bounded down the slope and entered the muddy water like a timid diver on a cold morning she realised that she had a full hand. There are 23 things which it is possible to do wrong in the drive, and she had done all of them."

PG Wodehouse

"When the squirrels and birds see us on the tee, they start scattering. We've set back the mating season in Texas by 90 days."

John Plumbley, coach of the Rice College Golf team

"The only time Nelson left the fairway was to pee in the bushes."

Jackie Burke on Byron Nelson

"Through years of experience I have found that air offers less resistance than dirt."

Jack Nicklaus on why he tees the ball up so high

"I had a stretch there for a few years where I played some golf that bordered on the Twilight Zone. I can remember getting upset that I had to putt."

Johnny Miller talking about his career in the mid-1970s when he won the 1973 US Open and the 1976 British Open

"At the Masters this year they raised the net at the end of the driving range by 20 feet. I'm one hopping it to the fence and he's flying it onto the Washington Road."

Paul Azinger on John Daly's driving ability

"If you want to try this shot you'd better have a backbone of steel, the strength of an ox and be younger than 30 years old."

Peter Alliss on Daly's phenomenal driving

"You'll be all right here, John. There are five courses and you're bound to hit one of them."

David Feherty to John Daly on the first tee at St Andrews

"When I first came out on Tour, I swung all out on every tee shot. My drives finished so far off line my pants were grass-stained at the knees."

Fuzzy Zoeller

"Mulligan: Invented by an Irishman who wanted to hit one more 20-yard grounder."
Jim Bishop, American journalist

"Hit it a bloody sight harder, mate."
Ted Ray on being asked by a pupil how he could hit the ball further

"A rough should have high grass. When you go bowling they don't give you anything for landing in the gutter, do they?"
Lee Trevino

"Drive for show, putt for dough."
Unattributed

"When I hit it, it goes downtown. The only problem is I don't know which town."
Rocky Thompson, US Senior Tour player

"The sand was heavier than I thought, and it only took me four swings to figure it out."
Johnny Miller at the 1974 US Open

"The limit of my ambition is not to lose my balance on the next backswing."
Mark James

OUT OF BOUNDS

"At least I'm keeping the balls in Bay Hill. Before I was hitting them all over Florida."
Sandy Lyle in 1991

"I'm hitting the woods just great, but I'm having a terrible time getting out of them."
Harry Toscano, American pro

"Heck, I wish they'd make the gallery ropes out of bounds. We're the only sport that plays in the audience."
Lee Trevino

"Hey, is this room out of bounds?"
Alex Karras, American footballer, to a startled employee after hitting a ball through a clubhouse window

"I can't say that I've played very well, Jack. It's taken me 69 holes to figure my problem out. But I've got it corrected now."
Johnny Miller to Jack Nicklaus on the 16th at Pebble Beach, in 1972, just before he shanked an approach shot

"What's over there, a nudist colony?"
Trevino after watching three partners all slice into a copse of trees

"Bing Crosby, who once lived on the 'slice' side of the 14th fairway at Pebble Beach, was reputed never to have had to buy a ball in his life."
Henry Longhurst

"The woods are full of long hitters."
Harvey Penick, University of Houston golf coach

"In golf, when we hit a foul ball, we got to go out and play it."
Sam Snead to legendary baseball player Ted Williams

"I could drive that hole if they put some dirt in front of the green."
John Daly after taking his Killer Whale driver and dumping the ball in the Swilcan Burn in front of the 1st green at St Andrews

"My game is so bad I gotta hire three caddies – one to walk the left rough, one for the right rough, and one down the middle. And the one in the middle doesn't have much to do."
Dave Hill

"Don't bother on my account, it was only an old ball."
Comedian Ted Ray to the driver of a JCB digging a trench

"I have discovered one important thing about the course, though – those big pine trees don't move."
Fuzzy Zoeller on Augusta

"The sooner they cut all these down for an edition of the *Guardian* the better."
Ffoulkes cartoon of a golfer caught behind a tree

"Ah yes sir, a slice, but a beautiful one."
   David Langdon cartoon – "Employee on tee to Boss"

Palmer: "Where do you think I should drop?"
Venturi: "Try Hawaii."
   Arnold Palmer after hitting his ball into the sea on the short 17th at Pebble Beach

THE GREEN

"The three worst words on a golf course, 'You're still away'."
   Unattributed

"A good player who is a great putter is a match for any golfer. A great hitter who cannot putt is a match for no one."
   Ben Sayers

"I don't have any big secret about putting . . . Just hit at it. It's either going to miss or go in."
   Ben Crenshaw

"When our putting is sour . . . then we are in honest, interminable, miserable trouble."
   Arnold Palmer

"You'll find that your worst putt will be as good as your best chip."
   Arnold Palmer recommending the use of the "Texas wedge" – a putter from off the green

"My putter had a heart attack the last 9 holes and just died on me."
   Lanny Wadkins

"Don't move, hole!"
   Lee Trevino

"The easiest shot in golf is the fourth putt."
   American humourist Ring Lardner

"If you're this close to the Pope and you can't putt he ain't gonna be able to do anything for me."
Sam Snead, hoping to get the Pope to bless his putter, to a golfing Monsignor in the Vatican who had never broken 100

"How often we hear it said of an otherwise fine golfer that he is lamentably weak on short putts . . . it seems logical to me that the player thus afflicted can get round the difficulty by not sending his approaches so near the hole."
Ring Lardner

"I always count two on the greens and thus avoid putting."
The Duke of Connaught to his perplexed opponent, Lionel Hewson, at the first hole of a game in the Curragh in 1904 (Hewson had six inches for his par, the Duke, 30 feet)

"Driving is a game of free swinging muscle control, while putting is something like performing eye surgery and using a bread knife for a scalpel."
Tommy Bolt

"I was thinking about how badly I needed to make the putt instead of what I needed to do to make the putt."
US Pro Kathy Whitworth on a four footer she missed to lose a tournament

"I have three-putted in over 40 countries."
Fred Corcoran

"There are no points for style when it comes to putting. It's getting the ball to drop that counts."
Brian Swarbrick, US pro

"Once you've had 'em, you've got 'em."
Henry Longhurst comment on the "Yips" which Bernhard Langer has disproved

"With the first movement of the putter, the golfer blacks out, loses sight of the ball and hasn't the remotest idea of what to do with the putter or, occasionally, that he is holding the putter at all."
Tommy Armour on the "Yips" which forced him out of tournament golf

"Yips don't seize the victim during a practise round. It is a tournament disease."

Tommy Armour

"It was what ultimately drove the pros out of the game to the teaching jobs at the country clubs, setting the balls on the tees for the girls in the Pucci pants who came down for their two free gift lessons of the summer."

George Plimpton on the "yips"

"I feel sorry for Casper. He can't putt a lick. He missed three 30-footers out there today."

Gary Player on Billy Casper, one of the best putters on the tour in his day

"The least thing upsets him on the links. He missed short putts because of the uproar of the butterflies in the adjoining meadows."

PG Wodehouse on "Mitchell Holmes" in "Ordeal by Golf"

"Most weeks he couldn't putt the ball into a two-car garage."

Journalist Dan Lauck on the less-gifted putter Larry Nelson

"How the devil can a man be expected to putt with all this traffic going up and down the Channel.

Easily distracted putter on the 6th at Deal

"That putter deserved to die."

Ken Green, tossing his putter into a pond

"I've never once seen the cup move towards the hole."

Henry Longhurst on NBC watching another putt come up short

"All I was seeking was that, on surveying a four-foot putt, a massive calm should automatically come over me instead of the impression that I was about to try to hit the ball with a live eel."

Henry Longhurst

"The best putters have almost invariably been slow movers. Walter Hagen took five minutes to reach for and lift a salt shaker, 45 minutes to shave. He just never rushed into anything."

George Low writing in 1983

"If I think I am going to miss and I hole it, then it's a bonus. If I think I am going to hole it and miss, then I am disappointed. So it is definitely better to think I am going to miss."

David J Russell, European tour pro

"I once shot a wild, charging elephant in Africa and it kept coming at me until it dropped to the ground at my feet. I wasn't scared. It takes a four-foot putt to scare me to death."

Sam Snead

"People tell me just to put the putter down and putt, but that's like telling a guy to go stand still by a rattlesnake – easier said than done."

Sam Snead at 62

"Even when times were good, I realised that my earning power as a golf professional depended on too many ifs and putts."

Gene Sarazen

"I'd chip it with a 5-iron before I used one of those things."

Ben Crenshaw on broom-handled putters

"We always considered it quite a feat to get down our six-to-eight footers, but now if a fellow misses from 40 feet he grimaces and agonises like a cowboy struck in the heart by an Indian's arrow."

Ben Hogan

"The putter . . . is a club designed to hit the ball partway to the hole."

Writer Rex Lardner

"Putting isn't golf. Greens should be treated almost the same as water hazards: you land on them, then add two strokes to your score."

Chi Chi Rodriguez

"He just told me to keep the ball low."

Chi Chi Rodriguez detailing some useful putting advice from his caddy

"The way I putted, I must have been reading the greens in Spanish and putting them in English."
Homero Blancas

"Gimme: An agreement between two losers who can't putt."
Jim Bishop

"The less said about the putter the better. Here is an instrument of torture, designed by Tantalus and forged in the devil's own smithy."
Tony Lema

"A devoted golfer is an anguished soul who has learnt a lot about putting just as an avalanche victim has learnt a lot about snow."
Dan Jenkins

"Would you like to know how to sink those putts? Just hit the ball a little closer to the hole."
Valerie Hogan to her husband Ben

"One time I sent off to the Ping factory and told them to send me the five ugliest putters they had; I just wanted to use something as ugly as my putting stroke."
Mark Calcavecchia

"My putter's got a small virus and I'm giving it Aspirin every night."
Fuzzy Zoeller

"I must have 30 putters at home and none of them works. They're all the same. They all let you down in the end."
A despairing Ian Woosnam

"Even a blind pig finds an acorn now and again."
Woosnam on putting well (at last)

"I could make it from everywhere. I was going to make long putts every tournament; I was going to make the field goals."
Tom Watson on how well he putted in his heyday

"The other one didn't float too well."
Craig Stadler on being asked why he was using a new putter

THE BODY

"How frequently have I persuaded patients who were never off my doorstep to take up golf and how rarely, if ever, have I seen them in my consulting rooms after."
Dr Alister MacKenzie, the great course designer

"I'm just a little fat guy who hasn't got a great swing."
South African John Bland

"Some guys hope to shoot their age. Craig Stadler hopes to shoot his waist."
Jim Murray

"We have so many small players out here on tour, that's why I look like Big Mama."
US Woman pro Joanne Carner

"Golfers find it a very trying matter to turn at the waist, more particularly if they have a lot of waist to turn."
Harry Vardon

"Tournament golf is an athletic pursuit, not merely a cross-country stroll."
Gary Player

"In Texas a Mr Moody Weaver in a practice swing used such force that he broke his leg in two places."
"The Golfer's Handbook"

"Lee likes to tell his amateur partners to play their putts to break towards the side of the hole Herman is standing, because he's so big the green will slope toward him."
Peter Jacobsen on Trevino and his caddy Herman Mitchell

"A little sweet tooth won't kill a man as long as you do 100 push-ups and eat your granola in the morning."
Gary Player, who despite appearances to the contrary, does have a sweet tooth

"You can't shape a golf swing if you're not in shape."
Bob Toski, golf instructor

"A doctor X-rayed my back and told me it looked like a clothesline with a load of wash on it."
Sam Snead on growing older

"The trouble with me is I can't turn, and when you can't turn, you look at your driver after you hit it because you think you left the head cover on."
Snead at 71

"Let me put it this way, I'm not expecting to lose weight. The doctor just told me to watch my weight, so I've got it up there where I can see it now."
Rives McBee when asked if he was gaining weight

"If I didn't have these I'd hit it twenty yards further."
"Babe" Didrikson Zaharias on her breasts

"At Darwin, Australia, in 1951, a lady, so excited by a successful shot, threw up her hands, stepped back and stumbled over her golf bag. She fell and broke her arms above the wrists."
"The Golfer's Handbook"

"I'm on steak now. With $200,000 a year there ain't no sense in eating rice and beans any more."
Chi Chi Rodriguez in 1970 explaining why he had put on some weight

"I've been too fat for too long. So I'm looking forward to starting an exercise, weightlifting and conditioning programme."
Craig Stadler in May 1990 (You'd be forgiven for wondering when we are going to see the results)

"It was brutal. I must have thrown up every 20 minutes for 9 hours."
Paul Azinger on chemotherapy

"How many times have you tried to make love to your wife and she has a headache. You don't count them. Anyway it's nothing that a few belts of vodka in the evening won't cure."

Fuzzy Zoeller on his back problems

"Any heart problem is serious, but it's not life threatening. Who's to say I'm not going to get run over by a bus going to the golf course today?"

Payne Stewart after the diagnosis of his heart condition

"To really lose weight playing golf, the best place to play is in Mexico. Go to any Mexican golf course, stop at every hole and drink the water. Within a week you'll have reached your desired weight."

Comedian Buddy Hackett

"The noise of the bone breaking was so loud that people standing 150 yards away told me later they they had heard it and thought it was a gunshot."

Richard Boxall, who broke his leg on the 9th tee of the 1991 Open at Birkdale

"If this had happened one hole later Boxie would have been the first man in Open championship history to go out in 34 and back in an ambulance."

Unattributed quip by Birkdale spectator

"I understand you have a weight problem. As you know, I have kept my weight exactly the same for years. I will be glad to send you my diet."

The rotund comedian Jackie Gleason in a telegram to Arnold Palmer

"I wish I was five inches shorter. My legs are going all over the place."

Nick Faldo on being tall (With his known dedication it's surprising he doesn't go for surgery to correct this vertical challenge)

"Colin and I have enough blubber to protect us."

Sandy Lyle on how he and Montgomerie deal with the cold at the Dunhill Cup in October

"This guy filled a glass with alcohol, set fire to it and then pushed the flaming glass into my back over and over again. Whether it's cured the trouble permanently I don't know, but it certainly took my mind off my backache."

Seve on being treated for back pains in Bangkok during the 1992 Johnnie Walker Asian Classic

"My idea of a diet is, if it tastes good, spit it out."
Roger Maltbie

Eighth Hole: Mind Games Par 4

Hole: 8th European Club
Par 4 412 yds
Designer: Pat Ruddy

Lefty Stackhouse. Not a name to be whispered in your best cathedral voice. Nor one which evokes images of cerebration, of a profoundly contemplative nature. Lefty would have entirely defeated the acolytes of the Inner Game. They would have been Sonny Listons to his Muhammed Ali, Custers to his Crazy Horse, daisies to his wedge.

Lefty's "Self Two" was a dark, Mephistophelean force, as dark as Sammy Davis Junior looking for a black cat in an underground coal hole. When "Self Two" was in control of the Stackhouse organism the "dogs of war" were loose. He had a disconcerting habit of punching himself when he failed to live up to his expectations. He failed a lot. Once, in a towering rage, he punched himself so hard he knocked himself cold.

If his right eye offended him he plucked it out. Well, not exactly, but if his right hand caused him to hook he would take it to the nearest tree and bash it repeatedly against the bark screaming, "Take that, that'll teach you." When he wasn't flagellating himself he took it out on his clubs, sometimes separately, sometimes the entire bag in one raging torrent of anger.

Mind you, he did give them fair warning of what they might expect. Teeing up he would talk to his clubs, admonishing them, cajoling them, and ultimately threatening them. To have been a club in Stackhouse's bag must have been a bit like being a Roman courtier during the reign of Caligula.

A handy journeyman pro he reserved his best moment for a piece of off-course terrorism. After a really bad round he walked over to his Model T Ford and began, almost dispassionately, to disassemble it, mouthing unrecognisable curses as he tossed away the doors, bonnet, seats and engine parts.

Naturally, this low-self esteem caused Lefty to drink like a camel before a long Sahara crossing. In one wartime event, the Knoxville Open, all he had to do was complete his final round to win a money prize (18 pros were competing for 20 prizes). An apocalyptic bender the night before meant that he could barely function after nine holes. He decided to nip into the clubhouse for a nap before finishing his round. By the time he woke up the field had moved on to the next tournament.

Not even "Freud on the Follow Through" could have helped Lefty Stackhouse.

THE INNER GAME

"Learning to get out of one's way is the purpose of the Inner Game."
   Timothy Gallwey, originator of the concept of the Inner Game of Golf

"I'm not an intellectual person. I don't get headaches from concentration. I get them from double bogeys."
   Tom Weiskopf

"I try to have peace of mind. If you have that, you are a mental millionaire. It doesn't cost anything."
   Chi Chi Rodriguez

"All the real greats in golf have displayed the mental discipline and precision of Zen masters."
   Jim Loehr, golf writer

"Every once in a while you have to let the greyhound catch the rabbit or he'll quit chasing it."
   Curtis Strange on the elusiveness of confidence

"I'm gonna get me one of those stares."
   David Graham commenting on the Jack Nicklaus "game face"

"Give me a player with a little talent and a great amount of desire and I'll pick him every time over a guy with a great amount of talent and a little desire."
   Sam Snead

"In golf, as in no other sport, your principal opponent is yourself. No one touches the golfer's ball but the golfer himself. If you slice your approach with your 5-iron into a luxurious patch of brier, you cannot slink out of responsibility for a rotten shot by turning to your adversary, as you can in tennis, and exclaiming 'Beautiful forehand, Reg'."

Herbert Warren Wind, eminent golf writer

"If you have to remind yourself to concentrate during competition, you've got no chance to concentrate."

Bobby Nichols, American pro

"Some days I felt like Superman and other days I found I was made of Jell-o."

Dave Marr

"In every tournament there are a few rounds of super golf; without a doubt they are played subconsciously."

Chick Evans, US pro

"The mind messes up more shots than the body."

Tommy Bolt

"Before the last round I called my wife and told her I had a 17-stroke lead over last place."

US pro Rod Funseth showing his total confidence in his game

"The person I fear most in the last two rounds is myself."

Tom Watson

"Most golfers prepare for disaster. A good golfer prepares for success."

Bob Toski

"Competitive golf is played mainly on a five and a half inch course, the space between your ears."

Bobby Jones

"I know I'm going to miss at least six shots a round. When I do, it's one down and five to go."

Walter Hagen

"When I'm standing over a shot I do occasionally visualise the clubhouse bar and I find that helps me. I also invented a thing for the BBC 2 series which concerns putting. When I stand over the putt I imagine that I have to make it in order to prevent an earthquake in Torquay."

Comedian and golfing philosopher Peter Cook

"Every day I tell myself this is going to be fun today. I try to put myself in a great frame of mind before I go out – then I screw it up with the first shot."

Johnny Miller

"You ask Chris Bonnington, while he is scaling the north face of K2 and is faced with a massive overhang, whether he is enjoying himself. When he gets to the top, that's when he enjoys himself."

David Feherty

"I feel that the unconscious mind has much better control than the conscious mind. The mind uses words and the muscles don't understand English."

Timothy Gallwey

"Golf is a compromise between what your ego wants you to do, what experience tells you to do and what your nerve lets you do."

Bruce Crampton

"Because I suck."

The disarmingly frank Nolan Henke on why he always ran down his game

ONE-UPMANSHIP

"If you want to beat somebody on the golf course, just get him mad."

Dave Williams, US pro

"We had the Cup on our table on the Aquitania coming over and we had reserved a place for it on the table going back."

Walter Hagen on the 1933 Ryder Cup (The Americans lost)

"My, you're hitting the ball beautifully. After you win this title, kid, you and I will go on an exhibition tour together."

Walter Hagen's surefire way of putting off an opponent who was outscoring him

"Sure I knew I had to win, but no man ever beat me in a play-off!"

Hagen after tapping in a nine footer to win the 1924 Open at Hoylake

"Hey, are you two still around? I thought you were gonna quit years ago."

Arnold Palmer's customary greeting to Gary Player and Jack Nicklaus at the Masters

"I have never used gamesmanship to win. Nor do I have much respect for a professional who claims he has been the victim of it. A man who complains about gamesmanship is a sissy."

Gary Player with a thoroughly reasoned argument against an accusation that is often levelled against him

"If he wants to fix traps then he shouldn't do it at my expense."

Johhny Miller on Gary Player who spent four minutes raking a bunker in the 1973 World Matchplay Championship while Miller waited to line up a vital putt

Harvey: "Of all the great teachers, they've chosen me to make this talk. How many great teachers do you suppose will be there?"
Helen: "Probably one less than you think."

Golf Coach Harvey Penick and his wife Helen before a lecture to a PGA convention

Player: "Having problems?"
Nicklaus: "Not really. I'm just seeing what sort of liberties I can take with the rough."

Nicklaus and Player during a practice round in which Nicklaus hardly kept the ball on the fairway

"I wanted to put some pressure on myself."

Phil Mickelson after conceding a 25-foot putt to an opponent for par and making a four-foot birdie putt

Jones: "Did you ever see a worse shot than that?"
Vardon: "No!"

The sole word spoken by Vardon in a round at St Andrews with Bobby Jones

"On the 10th he drew my attention to the fact that Olazabal was charging up the scoreboard. As if I couldn't see it for myself. Maybe he was trying to put me off."

Stephen McAllister on Colin Montgomerie at the 1990 Dutch Open. McAllister won!

"Gee, it's older than Hagen!"

Gene Sarazen being shown around a twelfth-century cathedral

"If your adversary is badly bunkered, there is no rule against your standing over him and counting his strokes aloud, with increasing gusto as their number mounts up; but it will be a wise precaution to arm yourself with a niblick before doing so, so as to meet him on equal terms."

Former British Amateur champion Horace Hutchinson, writing at the turn of the century

"My father was thinking of coming out for this tournament. Then when he found out who I had drawn as my first opponent, he changed his mind. He decided it wasn't worth a trip to Colorado just to watch me play one round."

The son of Bobby Jones (Robert Jones III) after being drawn against Nicklaus in the 1959 US Amateur Championship

"Good luck on this putt. They've got the original president of this club buried right there."

Lee Trevino to Dave Stockton as he faced a long putt over a bump

"If anyone beats 61 I'll call a steward's enquiry."

David Feherty after a great round in the 1991 Catalan Open

"You know, Claude, that's the first time I've ever birdied that hole."

Hogan to Claude Harmon after playing the 12th at Augusta (Harmon had just hit a hole-in-one)

"It was my first ever hole-in-one and I didn't even win the hole."

Albert Wilson, who halved the 12th at Woodhall Spa in England, with his friend Les Henshaw in 1982 (The odds against the feat were 1,844,874,304 to 1!)

"If the following foursome is pressing you, wave them through and then speed up."

Deane Beman, US PGA Tour Commissioner, giving good example

"No matter how hard I try, I just can't seem to break 64."

Jack Nicklaus

"After an abominable round of golf, a man is known to have slit his wrists with a razor blade and, having bandaged them, to have stumbled into the locker room and inquired of his partner, 'What time tomorrow?'"

Alistair Cooke

"It's like looking forward to falling off a cliff."

Steve Elkington on facing World No 1 Nick Faldo in the quarter-final of the 1993 Toyota World Matchplay Championships

"Well I guess all those years of practise finally paid off."

Jack Nicklaus Jr on breaking 50 for nine holes at the age of nine

"It is a law of nature that everyone plays a hole badly when going through."

Bernard Darwin

PRESSURE

"Always limp with the same leg for the whole round."

Henry Beard in "Mulligan's Laws"

"Greatness in golf is not achieved simply by striking the ball supremely well, but by doing so when it matters most."

Pat Ward Thomas, journalist and writer

"Everybody survives slumps . . . except maybe boxers. If they have a bad streak, they get knocked on their cans."

Tom Watson

"Everyone is watching your every move. Photographers take pictures of you doing everything; eating bananas; going to the toilet. It all adds up to the twitch factor which the young guys have to get used to."

Faldo on pressure from the press

"The history book will make you choke a lot quicker than prize money."

Jack Nicklaus

"When you're over a shot with a 4-iron into a crosswind to a green that runs away from you, and you've got alligators left and pterodactyls right, and you've got to make a birdie to make the cut or win the tournament, your major orifices pucker up, believe me."

Peter Jacobsen, American golfer, wit and writer

"Mediocrity knows no pressure."

Gary McCord

"My butterflies are still going strong. I just hope they are flying in formation."

Larry Mize on playing with a big third round lead

"Getting up in front of you teaching professionals makes me more nervous than anything except a three-foot downhill putt that breaks to the left on a slick green."

Harvey Penick to a seminar

"The pressure gets worse the older you get. The hole starts to look the size of a Bayer aspirin."

Gary Player after winning his first US Senior tour event in two and a half years

"We're all choking out there, but some choke less than others."

Gary Player

"I've always been in a situation in life where I had to win. As a kid life was very hard. There was pressure to live every day. So when I came on tour, maybe that pressure wasn't as great as it is for the other guys."

Calvin Peete, black American golfer

"Fear of success is the greatest single destroying factor in golf."
Pat Ward Thomas

"I used to think pressure was standing over a four-foot putt knowing I had to make it. I learned that real pressure was 65 people waiting for their food with only 30 minutes left on their lunch-hour break."
US pro Amy Alcott on waitressing in the off-season

"I have never felt so lonely as on a golf course in the midst of a championship with thousands of people around, especially when things began to go wrong and the crowds started wandering away."
Bobby Jones

"When I learned how to breathe I learned how to win."
Tom Watson on coping with pressure

"Tranquilisers make it possible for a golfer to relax at his favourite form of relaxation."
American writer Stephen Baker

"There's a lot of pressure playing golf for a living, and if you don't step back from it every now and again your brain will calcify and become crustier than an elephant's toenail."
Peter Jacobsen

"It's always hard to sleep when you've got a big early lead. You just lay there and smile at the ceiling all night."
Dave Stockton

"The basic problem was that I have never really liked the game . . . it is far too slow for me. I only liked fast moving games like boxing and rugby."
Max Faulkner on the game that gave him ulcers

"When we come down to the final holes, some people find it very . . . hard . . . to breathe."
Jack Nicklaus

"Three holes to play, and a birdie and two pars to win."
Nicklaus's recipe for contentment

"C'mon guys, it's not like coming down the stretch at a major. Good gracious, if you make a mistake you still have eleven other guys helping you."

Jack Nicklaus on the pressure that goes with the Ryder Cup

"We all choke, and the man who says he doesn't choke is lying . . . we all leak oil."

Lee Trevino

"A lot of guys who have never choked have never been in a position to do so."

Tom Watson

"Choking is only unfamiliarity with the situation. After you have been in a certain situation a few times you learn how to handle it."

Ken Venturi

"I wish they would come up with another word for it, because it has no similarity to having a piece of prime rib stuck in your throat. Now that's choking."

Peter Jacobsen

"Relax? How can anybody relax and play golf? You have to grip the club, don't you?"

Ben Hogan

"Everybody has two swings: the one he uses during the last three holes of a tournament and the one he uses the rest of the time."

US pro Toney Penna

"I gassed it."

Scott Hoch on three-putting the 18th from eight feet to lose the 1987 PGA Championship

"Peer pressure is a big, big thing out here. If you have had a bad score you don't hang around for people to ask you how you got on because that only makes it worse."

Colin Montgomerie

"It gets bigger and bigger until the inevitable happens and it pops."

Ronan Rafferty comparing confidence to a bubble in a bubble bath

PHILOSOPHY

"It's good to be the first one in the clubhouse with a low score. You can't bogey from the scoreboard."
Lee Trevino

"I'll be the better for this tournament. After all a smooth sea never produced a skilful sailor."
US Pro Mac O'Grady after a bad week at the office

"The ugliest words in the English language are 'what if'. The prettiest words are 'next time'."
Chi Chi Rodriguez

"If it is a journey it is also a round: it always leads back to the place you started from . . . golf is always a trip back to the first tee, the more you play the more you realise you are staying where you are."
Shivas Irons in Michael Murphy's novel "Golf in the Kingdom"

"A golfer must never be morbid. Perfect confidence and a calm mind are necessary for the success of every stroke."
Harry Vardon

"No man has mastered golf until he has realised that his good shots are accidents and his bad shots good exercise."
Eugene R Black, amateur golfer and Governor of the US Federal Reserve

"Golf brings out your assets and liabilities as a person. The longer you play, the more certain you are that a man's performance is the outward manifestation of who, in his heart, he really thinks he is."
Hale Irwin

"Few things draw two men together more surely than a mutual inability to master golf, coupled with an intense and ever increasing love for the game."
PG Wodehouse

"I'm not interested in the rounds of golf I've played. My best games are ahead of me . . . It is the promise of improvement that makes golf captivating."

Michael Bamberger, writer and caddy

"Some of the things I didn't have to be told as a rookie travelling pro were to keep close count of my nickels and dimes, stay away from whiskey, and never concede a putt."

Sam Snead

"It is possible by too much of it to destroy the mind; a man with a Roman nose and a high forehead may play away his profile."

Sir WA Simpson in "The Art of Golf", published in the 1880s

"Here's my philosophy of life. There's a verse in the Bible, it says 'Exult in tribulation – knowing that tribulation brings perseverance, and perseverance, character.'"

Corey Pavin

"The game comes out of the ocean, just like man himself."

Scottish teaching professional John Stark, quoted by Michael Bamberger

"The thrill of seeing a ball fly over the countryside, over obstacles – especially over a stretch of water – and then onto the green and into the hole has a mystic quality. Something in us loves that flight. What is it but the flight of the alone to the alone?"

Shivas Irons

"The respect you have for the game makes you want to stay away from it. The love you have for it brings you back."

Peter Teravainen on playing badly

"Serenity is knowing that your worst shot is still going to be pretty good."

Johnny Miller

"It is nothing new or original to say that golf is played one stroke at a time. But it took me many strokes to realise it."

Bobby Jones

"What other people may find in poetry or art museums, I find in the flight of a good drive – the white ball sailing up into the blue sky, growing smaller and smaller, then suddenly reaching its apex, curving, falling and finally dropping to the turf to roll some more, just the way I planned it."
Arnold Palmer

"The world of golf – although inhabited by millions of people playing thousands of courses in dozens of countries – is, in truth, a small village."
Michael Bamberger

"You are only out here to win. Second doesn't matter. Second is about as important as fifty-second. Winning is the reason you are playing."
Arnold Palmer

"It's a lot more cheerful and hopeful to be 70 years young than to be 40 years old."
Gary Player

"The bravest, stupidest race in the world, the unconvincible, inextinguishable race of golfers."
Writer Bernard Darwin

"If you ever feel sorry for somebody on a golf course, you better go home. If you don't kill them, they'll kill you."
Seve Ballesteros in 1984

"If I can see the ball I can hit it, if I can hit it I can hole it."
Arnold Palmer's philosophy

"Golf is not a funeral, though both can be very sad affairs."
Bernard Darwin

"If you think you can, or if you think you can't – you're right."
Deane Beman, US PGA Commissioner

"I owe everything to golf. Where else would a guy with an IQ like mine make this much money?"
Hubert Green

"You're only here for a short visit. Don't hurry, don't worry. And be sure to smell the flowers along the way."
   Walter Hagen

"Everyone gets wounded in the game of golf. The trick is not to bleed."
   Peter Dobereiner

"The slow play habit, let me say, is like a cigarette habit – it is so hard to break that a man is wisest not to begin it."
   Jack Nicklaus, who never went "Cold Turkey" to break his habit

"Whatever anyone may care to say about golf, at least one thing is mercifully certain, namely that it is a voluntary affair."
   Henry Longhurst

"A golf course is the epitome of all that is purely transitory in the universe, a space not to dwell in, but to get over as quickly as possible."
   French writer Jean Giraudoux

"Too few of us fully realise just what we have in golf, a game that provides small miracles of pleasure almost from the cradle to the grave."
   Hugh McIlvanney, writer and journalist

"The world conspires to flatter us; only golf trusts us with a cruelly honest report on our performance."
   John Updike

"I have always been a seeker. I have always wanted to know what the purpose of being here is, and where we're going. I think everybody looks for answers in life. Some people look a bit harder than others."
   South African golfer and committed Christian Wayne Westner

"Golf is a puzzle without an answer. I've never known how to play the game and I will die not knowing how to."
   Gary Player as a senior

"Golf, like Art, is a goddess whom we must woo from early youth if we would win her; we must even be born to her worship."
   H Rider Haggard

"Use it, never fight it. It will always get the better of you if you do."
   British Open winner (1923) Arthur Havers

"If you watch a game it's fun. If you play it, it's recreation. If you work at it, it's golf."
   Bob Hope

Ninth Hole: Hall of Fame Par 4

Hole: 9th County Louth (Baltray)
Par 4 422 yds
Designer: Tom Simpson

The Blessed Trinity may be top dogs in the afterlife but in that great golf course in the sky (not Delgany where some of the greens are actually below cloud level) the Great Triumvirate still reigns supreme. What chance had God, the Son of God and the Holy Spirit in their team medal-matchplay game with Vardon, Braid and Taylor (sponsored by Dunhill)? The Great Triumvirate had no desire to embarrass Their Deities but were finally goaded into accepting the challenge.

Now God may have made the world, but could he make a leering five-foot sidehill putt? The Son of God may have given his life to save the selfsame world but he was to find that there were no gimmes in the real world of competitive golf. No miracles allowed either. No "burning bushes" to clear a path after a Holy Ghostly duck hook into the jungle. No "moving in mysterious ways" by the Lord during Braid's backswing. The Rules of Golf are as emphatic as the Ten Commandments (just longer, more complicated and far more difficult to observe). Rule 9(1) is quite precise on help from an "agency outside the match". An attempt by God to utilise his miraculous powers (as previously witnessed in the parting of the Red Sea) in order to avoid a penalty drop for driving into Rae's Creek on the 12th in Augusta (where else would they play – for God's sake!!!) was nipped in the bud by the official referee (an old R&A man, Mr Beelzebub, a devil of a stickler for the Rules).

Despite having created the world in a mere seven days and seven nights God proved to be much more deliberate on the course, prompting a penalty from Mr Beelzebub for slow play as well as the acid observation that "if he'd taken as much time over Creation as he did over his putts the world mightn't be in the sort of mess it is today." (An unfair comment if ever there was one, Augusta's green are far more treacherous than Adam and Eve.)

A tailpiece (with apologies to Mr Beelzebub) . . . it was most amusing and encouraging for the spectators in the God vs Vardon encounter to see the Deity constantly straying from the straight and narrow and allowing a 4-hole lead to slip away in the closing stages of the round before he lost on the 18th. His immediate response was to compose an 11th Commandment, "Thou shalt not get caught" which, of course, has subsequently been wilfully misinterpreted.

IRELAND

CARR, JOE

"Stroke play is a better test of golf, but match play is a better test of character."

Joe Carr

"That Irishman is so popular in the United States that he could stand for President. What's more, he'd probably be elected."

Gene Sarazen on Joe Carr

"Everyone is studying golf technique like mad. Every young lad now aspires to be another Palmer or another Nicklaus. We may go centuries before we produce another playwright."

Joe Carr in the 1960s (He needn't have worried)

CLARKE, DARREN

"Augusta National, that's the Porsche of golf courses, isn't it?"

Darren Clarke, a player noted for his penchant for fast and expensive cars

"I used to watch Seve on TV when I was growing up and to go toe to toe with him two days running and eventually beat him, is a dream come true."

Clarke on his first tournament victory, the Belgian Open, October 1993

DARCY, EAMON

"Darcy takes the club back on the outside with his right elbow pointing at the sky . . . It would be natural enough to develop an instinctive arm jerk at Delgany, like the reflexes of a slack wire walker trying to keep his balance."
Peter Dobereiner, golf columnist

"No one has had a swing like Eamon since Quasimodo gave up golf to concentrate on bell ringing . . . Though he looks like he has learned his golf at the Thunderbirds Golf Academy, Eamon remains a deceptively fine player."
Bill Elliot

"Not changing my swing when I was younger."
Darcy on being asked what was the biggest mistake he'd ever made

FEHERTY, DAVID

TEN THINGS YOU OUGHT TO KNOW ABOUT DAVID FEHERTY
1. He once trained as an opera singer with a Polish woman in Belfast.
2. He is fed up with being reminded that he once trained as an opera singer with a Polish woman in Belfast.
3. He has been both a caddy and a pro on the PGA Tour.
4. He was voted "Most Sexy Sportsman" by a woman's magazine.
5. After he won the Italian Open in 1986 he sang a sparkling rendition of "Just One Cornetto" on BBC Radio 2's *Sunday Sport*.
6. He has suffered from, and beaten, the "yips".
7. His stated ambition in life is to make as much money as he can as early as he can so that he can retire (if he wants to).
8. Any Jack Nicklaus-designed golf course is his definition of "Hell on Earth".
9. If he weren't playing golf he says he would have been a "wringer-outer for a one-armed window cleaner".
10. Were he to rewrite the Rules of Golf he would insert a new rule: "You should be allowed to tackle your opponent."

FEHERTY ON FEHERTY

"I took up golf because I couldn't sing. I listened to a recording of myself and thought: 'No one is going to pay to listen to that.'"

"I really don't enjoy playing this game at all anymore. You would have to be a pervert to enjoy the sort of feelings that I went through out there."
After winning BMW International in 1989

"He couldn't hit a tiled floor with a bellyful of sick."
On a pro-am partner

"I played quite solidly until I got on the first tee."
David Feherty after a 77 at St Melion, one of his least favourite courses

"I was swinging like a toilet door on a prawn trawler."
After a bad round in South Africa

"I may be paired with them but I'm unlikely to be actually playing alongside them. In fact there's a danger they might decide to call me through, thinking that I'm part of the match behind."
On partnering John Daly and Ian Woosnam in the opening rounds of the 1993 British Open

"The great thing about Europe is you can make friends and have fun with them. In America you would come down to breakfast and find 12 different players sitting at 12 different tables. I instinctively thought: 'The hell with this.'"
On the US PGA Tour – some years before he finally joined it

"Even if he dived behind a bush and put a flowerpot over his head, I could still sense he was around and I'd drop a shot."
On the nerves induced by being watched by his father

"I considered beating the living daylights out of it but it's probably got a wife and snakelets."
On being bitten by an adder at the PGA Championship

"I have taken so many drugs I wouldn't pass a dope test. If you had a headache and stood next to me it'd go away."
On the painkillers he took for the bite

"Asking Nicklaus to redesign Augusta was like asking Andy Warhol to repaint the Sistine Chapel."

On his least-favoured golf course architect (Though he did praise the Nicklaus layout at Mount Juliet!)

"I went out there to play like Jack Nicklaus and ended up playing like Jacques Tati. It was farcical."

On failing to make the cut at the 1992 Cannes Open

"I saw a road runner and a coyote and I expected to see Bugs Bunny."

On his first impressions of the US tour in January 1994

"My ultimate ambition is to be able to retire from the game because it drives me berserk."

O'CONNOR JR, CHRISTY

"Some players will take the face off you if you try to talk to them during a tournament round. By contrast, I probably have encouraged a few too many people to approach me during a tournament."

Christy O'Connor Jr

"That 2-iron against Couples changed my life – it opened so many doors."

Christy O'Connor Jr

"You'll never be as good as your uncle."

Galway pro Bob Wallace in an exasperated effort to get a young Christy Jr off his back

"I kept out of all the broken beer bottles."

Christy O'Connor Jr on being asked to account for his round of 64 in the 1985 Open at Sandwich

"Did you really play all 18 holes?"

Reaction of Henry Cotton, whose record O'Connor beat

O'CONNOR SR, CHRISTY

"Christy is one of the most natural players I have ever seen."
Gary Player

"To watch Christy is to watch a craftsman at work."
Henry Cotton

"Tournament golf is a solitary calling, no less than writing or painting, and it needs uninterrupted dedication and application to succeed, but Christy never had the slightest wish to be excused his companionable responsibilities."
Peter Dobereiner

"While he was here I lost every penny I had to him."
Dr Billy O'Sullivan of Killarney, famous amateur international, on his many games with O'Connor

"Flowing, like fine wine."
Lee Trevino on Christy's swing

"Christy has as much rhythm as an old blues singer."
His friend and fellow pro Paddy Skerrit

"I could not have broken 80 from the places O'Connor got himself into; never at anytime in my life."
Byron Nelson after O'Connor's 65 in the second round of the 1969 Open at Lytham

RAFFERTY, RONAN

RAFFERTY ON RAFFERTY
"I tend to think of myself as the Stadler of the European tour. You know, the big fat brash fella who gives it a massive wallop and couldn't care two fiddler's tosses."
Rafferty (1984)

"It was like hearing your hero was gay. I was devastated."
Rafferty on the fact that his St Andrews Trophy partner Peter McEvoy didn't play the "big" 1.68" ball in 1981

"I love having kids and being with them. Five million people have them every month but when it's your own, it's different."

"Those guys who say they've had a great time out there, are having a theatrical response. You may grin up to the last minute if you're leading, but it's not wonderful fun."
   Rafferty on winning

"I probably did things in my youth which were wrong in the eyes of the gin-and-tonic swillers of the time. I didn't think they were wrong then, and if I was 15 now, I would probably tell them to get stuffed again."

"As far as I'm concerned I see the Irish Open as just another European tour event, and it didn't fit into my schedule."
   Rafferty explaining why he didn't play in his national Open for two consecutive years

OTHERS ON RAFFERTY
"It was like playing a computer. I have never seen such maturity in someone so young."
   Michael Bonnallack on Rafferty after losing to the then 16-year-old in the Amateur Championship

"When I travelled abroad with him for six weeks I thought, 'God is this guy immature,' but I had to keep reminding myself that he was only 17. He kept a water pistol and would shoot it at me in the car."
   Friend and fellow pro Roger Chapman

"He is still very much an individual. If 99 people say white, Ronan will say black, just for the hell of it."
   Roger Chapman on Rafferty in his late twenties

"He's as nice as pie at home, a real gentleman, but he can sprout horns with the press."
   Roger Chapman

"What he failed to mention to the Australian was that the toilet he had in mind was several thousand miles away in Cornwall."
   Journalist Joe Howard on Rafferty's remark to Craig Parry on the 10th hole, second day of the 1991 US Open. He walked off and didn't come back.

SMYTH, DES

"When the wolf gets you, you're gone. I remember seeing those teeth and I said to my friends the other day, that wolf nearly had me. I'm sure there are a lot of players with that wolf right up against their door but he's well out of my garden and I don't want to see him back again."
Des Smyth on missing cuts

"I'm a simple man. If I'm not feeling too good, I'll go in and have a bit of a sing-song and a few pints and that'll do me."

"All my career I've played my best golf from August till the end of the season – it takes me till then to get the alcohol out of my system and get down to taking golf seriously."

"To earn a million – who would have thought it? I've done it the hard way too, a thousand pounds here and a thousand pounds there."
On joining the European Tour "Millionaire's Club"

EUROPE

BARNES, BRIAN

"I need two Sherpas, one to carry my clubs, the other to carry me."
Barnes on the hot, mountainy Düsseldorf course where the German Open was played in 1991

"He's young, strong and supple and one heck of a player. He reminds me of myself at his age."
Barnes tongue-in-cheek comment on Steven Richardson

"I realise now that I should have worked harder at the game. My new resolve is to work harder . . . starting tomorrow."

"On occasion, he'd mark his ball with a beer can and ask attractive women in his gallery to recommend to him a good masseuse."
Michael Bamberger on Barnes

BALLESTEROS, SEVERIANO

BALLESTEROS ON BALLESTEROS
"I win with my heart."

"I am still young. When I am older there will be time to be careful."
Seve in 1976

"First I hit the ball, then I find the ball, and then I hit the ball again."
The young Seve on his style of play

"I won't change. If you think I do then come to me and say 'Where is Seve Ballesteros?' I will understand."
Seve after winning the 1979 Open, his first Major

"My problem is that I try too hard sometimes, that I am too hard on myself. I seek perfection and despite the fact that I know such a thing is impossible in this game, I cannot help but go on searching for it."
Seve in 1988

"I make more miracle shots than anyone else because I take more risks . . . I don't like going backwards."
Seve on the many problems he's had off the tee

"I am just a lucky golfer, no?"
Seve to journalists who underrated the "car park champion" of the 1979 Open

"Sometimes I think the only way the Spanish people will recognise me is if I win the Grand Slam and then drop dead on the 18th green."
Seve on being a prophet without honour . . .

"I feel like a criminal who has done something very bad."
Seve after missing the cut in three successive PGA tournaments

"I am not playing well but I don't know whether I am not playing well because I have no desire or I have no desire because I am not playing well."

OTHERS ON BALLESTEROS

"He stalks the world's fairways like some predatory animal, confident that in his patch of sporting jungle he is the king."
Bill Elliot

"He goes after a golf course like a lion at a zebra. He doesn't reason with it; he tries to throw it out of the window or hold its head under water till it stops wriggling."
Jim Murray, sports writer

"Seve, unless his putting stroke deserts him, should become the richest Spaniard since Queen Isabella."
Jim Murray after Seve's 1979 Open win

"Oh Severiano, you have left the English and Americans destroyed like eagles."
A ballad sung for Seve in his native Pedrena

"He's a gorilla off the tee. He's out of control, certainly, but that goes with being young."
Billy Casper

"I once told Seve that some players get frightened and back off when they get into a position to win. He didn't believe me. He just looked at me kind of funny."
Dave Musgrove, one-time Seve caddy

"When Seve gets going its like matching a Model T Ford against a Ferrari. He plays shots which the rest of us can't even imagine."
Ben Crenshaw

"The game lives in him. He can create atmosphere wherever he is. That's what charisma is about."
Tony Jacklin

"He's nearer 40 than 30 and everyone, no matter who, only has so many bullets in the gun."
Peter Alliss (1994)

FALDO, NICK

"I would be too sexy to wear shorts. There would be trouble from the gallery. And anyway, Monty (Colin Montgomerie) in shorts, no thanks."
Faldo on the suggestion that shorts be worn in the 1993 Johnny Walker World Championship

"All the people who said I was wrong know that they said it. Now it's a question of whether they've got the balls to turn around and admit I was right."
Faldo on completely changing his swing in the mid-1980s

"I'd be interested to know if Jack Nicklaus has ever come home, picked the clubs out of the back of the car and just thrown them straight into the garage wall."
Faldo on frustration with his play

"Subjective but has a great desire to achieve greatness . . . clear-minded, strongly egotistic . . . a lack of modesty and a tendency to loneliness."
Characteristics identified in a study of Faldo's handwriting

"(He has) that demon in there jabbing at his vitals with a pitchfork. After all, without his demon Faldo would be just another golfer."
Peter Dobereiner

"Faldo is as much fun as Saddam Hussein."
Scott Hoch (So he didn't crack any jokes on the 11th at Augusta in 1989!)

"There is something, we feel, not quite British about wanting to win so badly that it hurts."
Journalist Martin Vousden on a possible cause of popular ambiguity towards Faldo

"I've known Nick for years yet I don't think I know the real Nick Faldo."
Sandy Lyle

"Like playing by yourself, except it took an hour longer."
Steve Pate on playing with Faldo in the final round of the 1992 Open

"If a golfer is forced to dress like a plonker the chances are that he will fall victim to the Payne Stewart syndrome and play like a plonker."
Peter Dobereiner on the Faldo dress code in the mid-1980s. (Stewart does OK though!)

"Faldo gets involved in controversies as often as a child walks through puddles."
John Hopkins, Times *Golf Correspondant*

FAULKNER, MAX

"Max Faulkner, Open Champion."
Autographs given by Faulkner after the second round of the 1951 Open, which he duly won

"Perhaps the truth was that Max, like so many extroverts, was never quite as colourful as he seemed. I often thought there was a rather lonely figure in there, longing to get out."
Peter Alliss

JAMES, MARK

"I couldn't live anywhere other than in Britain, but I'd quite like it to be parked off the coast of Australia."
Mark James

"I would like to be remembered as someone who won 12 Major championships in his career."
James, with tongue in cheek

LANGER, BERNHARD

"Why was I so uptight? I could chip and hit pitch shots without problems. Why not putt? I knew it was there. I kept telling myself it was."
Langer on conquering the "yips"

"I think you can be a Christian and still have a killer instinct."
Langer on his very public Christianity

Langer: "How far have you got?"

Monty: "124 yards to the green, plus 26 on – that's 150 yards into the breeze, a 7-iron."

Langer: "Where are you taking your yardage from – the front or the back of the sprinkler head?"

Langer and Colin Montgomerie in the 1991 Ryder Cup fourball (A sprinkler head is about nine inches in diameter)

"When he practises alone Langer can hold up a fourball."

Tour caddy Dave Musgrove on the time Langer spends around greens during a practice round

LYLE, SANDY

"Don't talk to me I'm hurting. Brain, thick, dumb, shit."

Sandy Lyle after bogeying the last 5 holes in the third round of the 1993 US PGA

"Try to slow your swing down to a blur."

Advice to comedian Tom O'Connor from Lyle

MONTGOMERIE, COLIN

"I know I'm part of a public entertainment, but if you walk into anyone's office and they are looking at some bad figures on the balance sheet, they're not smiling too much either."

Montgomerie on why he scowls a lot on golf courses

"I think that as golfers we are overpaid. It's unreal and I have trouble dealing with the guilt sometimes. We talk about tragedy on a golf course when someone misses a putt but that's not tragedy. Tragedy is what's happening in Bosnia."

Montgomerie on money and conscience

"No longer the baby of the family since his wife Eimear gave birth last March."

Unidentified journalist on Montgomerie

"(The temper of) a warthog recently stung by a wasp and a face like a bulldog licking piss off a nettle."

David Feherty on Montgomerie's less salubrious attributes

"Perhaps he's watched too many episodes of *One Foot in the Grave*."
Peter Alliss, who clearly shares Feherty's opinion of Monty's lugubrious qualities

OLAZABAL, JOSE MARIA

"When I was ten I had never heard of Seve."
Olly giving the lie to the myth that he always idolised Ballesteros

"In Spain we have a saying which is that before you can reap you must first sow the seeds. The seeds are all now planted. I now feel that I am out of Seve's shadow."
Olazabal mixing his metaphors

"I have been trying so hard for so long that it was like staring at a grey prison wall. Now I am on the other side and it is all green with trees, lakes and flowers."
Olazabal after winning his first major championship, the US Masters, in April 1994

VARDON, HARRY

"Braces seem to hold your shoulders together."
Vardon on why he wore them when he played

"Imperturable, taciturn, he seldom smiled on the course, but then he seldom scowled either. He never threw a tantrum, never gave an alibi. He just came to play."
The great golf writer, Charles Price, on one of the first great professionals

"If a dog crossed the tee in front of him while at the top of his swing he would be able to judge whether the dog ran in any danger of its life. If it did he would stop his club; if it didn't, he would go through with the shot, without pulling or slicing."
Andrew Kirkcaldy

WOOSNAM, IAN

"I worked as a barman, a bouncer and I even planted trees just to get enough to pay for my next tournament."
Ian Woosnam

"At least I'm consistent."

Woosnam after his second consecutive 82 at St Melion in 1991, an understandable enough reaction to his great US Masters a few weeks earlier

"His swing is just one sweet flowing motion without any bits and pieces."

Bob Torrance on his pupil

"Woosnam is a product of the oriental art of miniaturising professional golfers, but there is nothing bonsai about the scale of Woosnam's golf."

Peter Dobereiner

"I dread the day he's out of golf, when he doesn't have anything left to fight for."

Harold Woosnam, Ian's father

UNITED STATES OF AMERICA

AZINGER, PAUL

"Lets face it, I'm blessed. I have an inner peace, a faith in the Lord, a wonderful wife, two kids, great parents and so many friends. And golf's been good to me."

Azinger on coming to terms with cancer

"If I cared about the way I looked, I would have changed my grip. But you don't have to be technically perfect to do it right."

Azinger on his unorthodox swing

"We just didn't ham and egg it."

Azinger after he and Payne Stewart lost 7&5 to Woosnam and Langer during the 1993 Ryder Cup foursomes

"When he turned professional back in 1981 it was as though the village idiot had announced his intention of investigating the possibility of a career in astrophysics."

Bill Elliot on Azinger

COUPLES, FRED

"When you guys want to talk to me you go to a golf course, so I stopped going to golf courses. Anyway, I'm lazy."
Couples telling the press why he was out of practice

"He'd probably be like that if he was writing a poem. He'd spend two days at that and want to make it perfect. I'm not like that. I'd be happy with 'Roses are red, violets are blue, I'm at Augusta and so are you.'"
Couples contrasting his own temperament with that of Nick Faldo

"He just steps up to the golf ball, takes a deep breath to relax, takes it back, and whomps it. Then he goes and finds it and whomps it again. And when you add up the whomps, the total is usually lower than that of the other 143 whompers."
Peter Jacobsen

"He's now known as Fred Singles."
American broadcaster Bernard Guirk after Couples's divorce

"I'd like to have Fred Couples's face. Fred Couples's body, Fred Couples's swing . . . and Fred Couples's ex-wife's bank account."
Rocky Thompson, US Senior Tour player

DALY, JOHN

DALY ON DALY
"It was probably the most important drive of my career."
Daly on his 600-mile drive to Crooked Stick, Indiana, after getting Nick Price's place in the 1991 PGA

"As soon as I tee up my ball, Squeaky says 'Kill' and I just kill it."
Daly on "Squeaky" Medlin – Price's caddy whom he borrowed

"She fooled everybody. I go with a girl for nearly two years and I don't know how old she is and that she's got a kid. It makes me look stupid."
On discovering at the Johnny Walker World Championship in Jamaica, Dec 1991 (in which he finished last) that his girlfriend Bettye Fulford was not 29 but 39, was married and had a child

"I tell them 'OK, if you got a hundred grand in your pocket, let's go.'
And that's the end of that."
On being approached by people who reckon they can outdrive him

"I don't drink any more, just beer."
Daly, before going into alcohol rehab

"I've heard the winner of the Masters hosts the dinner. If I ever won
it there would be no suits, no ties and McDonalds."

"A year ago the only people watching me were my caddy, the
scorekeeper and the guy carrying the sign."
Talking about the crowds following him at the Masters

OTHERS ON DALY
"He's longer than Fred Couples. He's longer than Greg Norman. He's
even longer than 'War and Peace'."
Bob Verdi, Chicago Tribune

"By the time we walk up to his drive, my clothes have gone out of
style."
Daly's good friend Fuzzy Zoeller

"I'll just sit here in the shade and wait for your ball to come down."
Zoeller

"Compared with pistol packing college football players who shoot up
their dorms, and countless pro athletes who have been convicted of
drunk driving, Daly sounds like a choir boy."
*Writer Thomas Boswell comparing Daly's alleged misdeeds to those
of others*

"I wouldn't mind if he doesn't come back."
*Mike Hughesdon, BBC commentator, on Daly, May 1993, after the
1992 Open*

"I hope we see John Daly back next year."
Mike Hughesdon, September 1993, after the 1993 Open

"Daly's divots go further than I can drive the ball."
David Feherty

"John Daly is just ridiculous with his length. I couldn't hit it where he hits it on a runway."
Fred Funk, US pro

"I'm a very fast walker and if I wanted to talk to him I had to jog . . . I didn't want to talk that bad."
Bruce Lietzke on Daly's walking pace

Floyd, Raymond
Floyd: "What's that below?"
Passenger: "That's the Forth."
Floyd: "Hell of a carry."
Floyd in a light aircraft flying over the Firth of Forth

"If I could make a pact with the devil, I'd take a British Open and happily retire the next day."
Floyd on his ambition to complete the modern professional Grand Slam

"If a great swing put you high on the money list, there'd be some of us who would be broke."
Floyd on his eccentric but effective style

"The game was easy for me as a kid and I had to play a while to find out how hard it was."

"Those are guys who realise how lucky we have all been, who appreciate what golf has given us. There's a whole lot of folks that come into these locker rooms nowadays who don't appreciate what they've got here."
Floyd on the players on the Senior tour

"I always travel first class – that way I think first class and I'm more likely to play first class."

"They call it golf because all the other four-letter words were taken."

HAGEN, WALTER

"Give me a man with big hands, big feet and no brains and I will make a golfer out of him."
Walter Hagen

"Well fellas, who's gonna come second?"
Hagen's regular greeting to his fellow competitors before a tournament

"I don't want to die a millionaire, just live like one."

"Golf has never had a showman like him. All the professionals who have a chance to go after the big money today should say a silent thanks to Walter each time they stretch a cheque between their fingers."
Gene Sarazen on Walter Hagen

HOGAN, BEN

"You'll never get anywhere fooling around those golf courses."
Hogan's mother when he was sixteen

Hogan: "What equipment do you play?"
Player: "Spalding, Mr Hogan."
Hogan: "Why don"t you ask Mr Spalding?"
Gary Player being rebuffed after seeking advice from the irascible Hogan

"Selecting a stroke is like selecting a wife. To each his own."
Hogan on putting

"His legs simply were not strong enough to carry his heart around."
Comment on Hogan's comeback in the Los Angeles Open of 1950 after the car accident which almost killed him. He lost a play-off to Sam Snead.

"You play a game with which I am unfamiliar."
Bobby Jones's famous compliment to Hogan (Subsequently said to Nicklaus)

"Hogan came closer to dehumanising the game than anyone else has ever done."
Pat Ward Thomas

"Watching Hogan . . . we were almost convinced, that if he hit a shot into a bunker, well, that's the way the hole should be played."
US writer Robert Sommers

"If he were a judge I believe he would give you the benefit of the doubt on your first offence, but he'd never let you off the hook twice. He would condemn you to death without batting an eyelash."
Sports promoter Fred Corcoran

"I am just sorry that no one knows more about him. But then, perhaps he has hidden his memoirs, buried them in capsules which will be opened when the Martians get here in about five million years, and they will discover the Thoughts of Chairman Ben, Golfer."
Peter Alliss

IRWIN, HALE

"A picture book golfer with the face of a PhD candidate."
John Updike

JONES, ROBERT TYRE "BOBBY"

"You can only hope to be the best of your time."
Jones on whether he was the greatest golfer ever

"I'll never have another chance to win both the British and American Open Championships in the same year."
Bobby Jones in 1926. How wrong he was!

"I wasn't quite certain what had happened or what I had done. I only knew that I had completed a period of most strenuous effort, and that at this point, nothing more remained to be done."
Jones after winning the fourth leg of his great 1930 Grand Slam, the US Amateur

"I expect to play golf, but just when and where, I cannot say now."
The key phrase in Jones's victory speech, which became his golfing valedictory

"It is not our intention to rig the golf course so as to make it tricky. It is our feeling that there is something wrong with a golf course which will not yield a score in the sixties to a player who has played well enough to deserve it."
Jones on Augusta, which he and Dr Alister MacKenzie designed

"He had supernatural strength of mind."
Ben Hogan

"My, but you're a wonder, sir."
An awestruck young caddy after a spectacular shot from Jones

"There were no worlds left to conquer for Bobby Jones."
Herbert Warren Wind on the legacy of the 1930 Grand Slam

"I am, by nature, a hero worshipper, as, I guess, most of us are, but in all the years of contact with the famous ones of sport I have found only one that would stand up in every way as a gentleman as well as a celebrity, a fine, decent, human being as well as a newsprint personage, and who never once, since I have known him, has let me down in my estimate of him. That one is Robert Tyre Jones Jr."
Paul Gallico in his valedictory "Farewell to Sport"

KITE, TOM

"It's hard to take a chance when you can't reach the green in the first place."
Kite on his relative lack of length off the tee

"It bugged the living daylights out of me."
On what it was like to face repeated questions about never having won a Major

"I didn't tie with him, he tied with me."
Kite after he tied with his old adversary Ben Crenshaw for an NCAA title

"If Tom has a 50-gallon drum of potential, he's using 48 gallons of it."
Peter Jacobsen

NICKLAUS, JACK

NICKLAUS ON NICKLAUS
"After viewing me in action in this swing around California, very few established pros had packed their bags in panic and headed for home."
Nicklaus on his first months on the pro Tour

"During the 1970s, I wasn't a good striker of the ball at all. Oh, sure, I won a lot of tournaments."
(Eight Majors, to be precise, during that decade)

"I want to go home and throw up."
After a 75 at the Open in Muirfield (1992)

"I'm having a problem with being 50."

"I never take my golf home. When I win, my celebration is with my family. We don't open champagne because I don't like it and have never seen the sense in getting drunk."

OTHERS ON NICKLAUS
"I never thought his short game was very good. Of course he hit so many greens it didn't make a difference."
Tom Watson on Nicklaus in 1981

"Like Jack Nicklaus, very good and very slow."
Robert di Vicenzo on the food in a restaurant

"Jack Nicklaus has become a legend in his spare time."
Chi Chi Rodriguez

"He wouldn't three putt a supermarket parking lot."
Dave Hill

"The greatest player who ever wore a slipover shirt."
Dan Jenkins

"I felt like a peashooter against a cannon."
Clive Clark after a round with Nicklaus

"In Ohio, Nicklaus would win a popularity contest over a parley card of Mother Teresa, Johnny Carson and Elvis back from the dead."
Peter Jacobsen

"I enjoyed being in the last group of the day behind Nicklaus. The only trouble was Jack Tuthill (the tournament director) kept taking the pins off the greens once Nicklaus played through."
Lou Graham

"I did my best, but chasing Nicklaus is like chasing a walking record book."
Tom Weiskopf after losing another finish to the Golden Bear

"Most of the time he plays with the timidity of a middle-aged spinster walking home through a town full of drunken sailors, always choosing the safe side of the street."
Peter Dobereiner

"The difference between Jack and me is that when I got to the top of the mountain in 1974 and 1975, I said, 'Hey, it's time to stop and check out the view.' Whenever Jack reaches the top of a mountain, he starts looking for another."
Johnny Miller

PALMER, ARNOLD

"One good thing about shooting the way I've been shooting. You get to play early while the greens are still smooth."
Palmer towards the latter part of his career

"Arnold Palmer could never repay you people or the game of golf for what it has meant to him."
Palmer on being made a Memorial tournament honoree

"No matter what happens I can always dig ditches for a living."
During a losing streak

"Palmer not only makes a golf tournament seem as dangerous as an Indianapolis 500, but he crashes as often as he finishes first."
Mark McCormack on one of his earliest clients

"Here lies Arnold Palmer. He always went for the green."
Mark McCormack's suggested epitaph for his famous client

"He can hitch up his pants or yank on a glove and people will start oohing and aahing. When I hitch up mine, nobody notices."
Jack Nicklaus

"I like Arnold Palmer. I think he's a helluva guy. I don't think he feels the same way about me."
Nicklaus

"He'd go for the flag from the middle of an alligator's back."
   Lee Trevino

"Arnie has more people watching him park the car than we do out on the course."
   Trevino

"The two golfers are as dissimilar in manner as the commander of a mechanised army and the leader of a great cavalry brigade, as the rifle to the broadsword."
   Pat Ward Thomas on Palmer and Hogan

"Playing with Palmer occasionally makes me nervous. I don't mind when he criticises my swing and my grip, but when he starts lifting me in and out of the golf cart, that's too much."
   Bob Hope

Pavin, Corey

"Corey Pavin is a little on the slight side. When he goes through the turnstile, nothing happens."
   Jim Moriarty, Golf Digest, *1984*

"He manufactured shots, he showed great skill and nerve, and when asked to speak, he strung words together as if he'd actually been to school."
   Peter Alliss on Pavin's win in the 1993 World Matchplay

"This must be the swing of the future, for I sure as hell haven't seen anything like it in the past."
   Charles Price on Corey Pavin's swing

"If my son wants to learn golf I'll send him to Corey."
   Nick Price

Snead, Sam

"Where I lived, near Bald Knob, the roads got littler and littler until they just ran up a tree. Big cities were something I'd just heard rumours about . . . The valleys are so narrow that the dogs have to wag their tails up and down."
   Snead on his birthplace

"The only reason I played golf was so I could afford to go hunting or fishing."

"It's all right to put all your eggs in one basket – if you've got the right basket."

"Before I play, I like a slow drive to the course with slow music on the radio and a light touch on the steering wheel."

"I'm really 15 years younger than my birth certificate shows. In Virginia, we don't count the years you go barefoot."

"I am only scared of three things: lightning, a side-hill putt and Ben Hogan."

"I swing just as hard but I walk slower and get to the ball quicker."
Snead on losing distance off the tee as he was getting older

"When I dine with Mr Snead he always suggests that I order as if I was expecting to pay for it myself. I have known many great destroyers of money, but Mr Snead is not among them."
George Low on Snead's legendary tightness with money

"If the legend is true that Sam keeps all his wealth buried in tomato cans, the designated site must be an area as big as Fort Knox."
Robert Trent Jones

TREVINO, LEE

TREVINO ON TREVINO
"My family was so poor the lady next door gave birth to me."

"By the time I was five I was out in the fields . . . I thought hard work was just how life was. I was 21 years old before I knew Manual Labour wasn't a Mexican."

"I can't keep my mouth shut for four hours around a golf course. If I did I'd get bad breath."

"I'm very lucky. If it wasn't for golf, I don't know what I'd be doing. If my IQ had been two points lower, I'd have been a plant somewhere."

"Too many drunks grab your hand and hold onto it. I have a quote for them: 'I'm not in love with you, sir. Let go.' That usually stops them."
Trevino on why he avoids clubhouse bars

"My wife's got a broken wrist, we've got a ten-week-old baby and our dog's pregnant. I came out here to rest."
During the 1969 Byron Nelson Classic

"It's one of those years. Jimmy Carter had four of them, so I don't feel so bad."
In 1981 after missing the cut in the Masters and US Open and being disqualified in the PGA

"Everybody thought I was an Italian . . . it seemed to me we were in the Italian capital of the world. So my gallery started getting bigger and bigger and the suits darker and darker. By the 18th, even the Godfather was there."
During the 1967 US Open at Baltusrol, New Jersey where he showed on the leader board for the first time in a major

"A walking 1-iron."
On the tall slim Ken Brown

"My wife doesn't care what I do when I'm away as long as I don't have fun."

"I should have hit a 1-iron that day, not even God can hit a 1-iron."
On being struck by lightning

"Personally, if I'm on the course and lightning starts I get inside fast. If God wants to play through, let him."

"Couldn't have worked out better, I didn't even need to change the names on the towels."
On marrying a woman named Claudia in 1983. It was also the name of his previous wife.

OTHERS ON TREVINO
"He makes Joan Rivers sound like Calvin Coolidge."
Bob Hope

"If he didn't have an Adam's apple he'd have no shape at all."
Gary Player

"Lee's got more lines than the Illinois railroad."
   Fuzzy Zoeller

"He's done it all with a swing that suggests a lumberjack going after the nearest redwood."
   Journalist Curry Kirkpatrick

"Trevino, so broad across he looks like a reflection in a funhouse mirror, a model of delicacy around the greens and a model of affable temperament everywhere."
   John Updike

"You don't have a relationship with Lee. Trevino is a very private person. And Trevino never really goes to dinner with anybody. He has room service."
   Jack Nicklaus

WADKINS, LANNY

"He's the most tenacious player I've ever seen. You put a pin in the middle of a lake and Lanny will attack it."
   US Pro John Mahaffey

WATSON, TOM

"My private life is nobody's business but mine. Some players get a big kick out of telling the world what they've got. I don't. I don't go much for those in-depth interviews that want to know the colour of your curtains and how many times you make love to your wife."

"I met some doctors and they told me how much they envied my life. Gosh, if only they knew how much I envy them. They contribute so much to life. Me? I don't know."

"Charisma is winning major championships."
   Watson, who has often been accused of lacking it

"It's like putting furniture together. The parts are there, but the glue is still a little wet."
   Tom Watson on his game in 1991 at the Masters

"Watson scares me. If he's lying 6 in the middle of the fairway, there's some kind of way he might make a 5."
Lee Trevino

"To call him complex would be to call Rubik's Cube slightly taxing."
Writer Larry Dorman

"Tom Watson . . . pensive Tom Sawyer, who, while the other boys were whitewashing fences, has become, politely but firmly, the best golfer in the world."
John Updike, writing in 1980

"Any self-respecting tournament wants to be won by Tom Watson."
Journalist Jim Murray

"I have to say on a personal level that I have never warmed to Tom as a person. I found him too dour."
Gary Player

"When you drive into the left rough, hack your second out into a greenside bunker, come out within six feet of the hole and sink the slippery putt – when you do that, you've made a Watson par."
Andy Bean

ZOELLER, FUZZY

"When your name is Zoeller, and so many things are done in alphabetical order, you expect to be last."
Fuzzy Zoeller

"When I catch my driver and Fuzzy catches his 1-iron, I can get within thirty yards of him."
Hale Irwin

THE ANTIPODES

GRAHAM, DAVID

"My golf? It's currently on vacation until I become a Senior in 1995. But thanks for asking."
David Graham in 1992

LOCKE, BOBBY

"That son of a bitch Locke was able to hole a putt over 60 feet of peanut brittle."
Lloyd Mangrum

"This guy from the bush duck-hooks every shot, including his putts."
Unattributed American quote

MARSH, GRAHAM

"Marsh, as befits a former teacher of mathematics, seems to go round golf courses with a pair of compasses, a protractor, dividers and a slide rule."
"Laddie" Lucas

NORMAN, GREG

"He looks like one of the guys they used to send after James Bond."
Dan Jenkins on the young Norman

"When I won, Bruce said 'Welcome back'. That was the nicest thing anybody ever said to me."
Norman after he beat Bruce Lietzke in a play-off for the 1992 Canadian Open, his first victory for over two years

"Shit, it owes me about four."
Norman after being asked did fate owe him a second Major to add to his Open victory in 1986

"I have come home from Augusta, or from the US Open, or from the US PGA Championship, and I've gone down to the beach and flat cried until about three or four o'clock in the morning."
The Great White Shark on some of his most famous disappointments

"In my entire career I have never gone round a course and never mishit a shot. Every drive was perfect, every iron was perfect. I was in awe of myself."
After his final round 64 to win the 1993 British Open

"It's . . . different. I'd swear the Air Force used a couple of the fairways for bombing runs. Out of 18 holes there are 11 that I like very very much. The others I'd rather not play."
Speaking about Royal St Georges, Sandwich, before he won his second Open there

"You have to use your head here. This is the world championship of imagination. And I love it."
An alternative view of the same course

"You've just played the greatest round of golf that I've ever seen."
Langer to Norman after his 64 at Sandwich

PLAYER, GARY

"It's a funny thing, the more I practise the luckier I get."
Gary Player after being asked a question about a "lucky" bunker shot

"I wear black. I loved Westerns and the cowboys always looked good in black."

"I believe that if a man takes care of himself, then, all things being equal, he should be as competent a golfer at 50 as he was at 30."
Player on his legendary fitness

"When you come up over a hill it's always a relief to see Gary on the fringe and not in the bunker."
Jack Nicklaus on Player's prowess from the sand

"This guy is grinding even when he's making a ten."
Lee Tevino on Player's application

"Sometimes he carries his positive thinking too far – he's the only guy I know who can shoot 80 and say he hit the ball super."
David Graham on Player
"If he doesn't have an obstacle to clear he will erect one to keep up his interest, and at positive thinking he could give Norman Vincent Peale two a side."
US journalist Nick Seitz

PRICE, NICK

"I hate the word 'Nice'. Everyone says, 'Oh he's such a nice guy.' Nice is such a horrible word, because its not descriptive enough. It is a compliment but I'd rather be known as a warm, friendly person than as a nice guy."

"Sometimes you try to figure out what you're doing right, but I'm just going to say to hell with it, and keep going."
   Price after winning the 1994 Honda Classic

"The best reason for playing is that Nick Price isn't."
   Davis Love III, commenting before an event during Price's great 1993 season

"I thought I was playing well and Nick made me look like a 27-handicapper."
   Greg Norman at the 1993 Western Open

"He's playing well, he's putting well and he's had luck on his side. Makes you sick, hey?"
   Faldo on Price who won the Sun City Challenge in December 1993 by 12 shots

THOMSON, PETER

"If you walked in on Thomson at home, unannounced, you'd be just as likely to find him reading Arthur Koestler, or listening to Gustav Mahler. A well-rounded man is Peter Thomson . . . "
   Peter Alliss

"He was a very over-rated golfer but I would say he was the best I have ever seen with the small golf ball on a firm links course. That was his stage."
   Gary Player on the five times Open Champion

"We Americans always liked to win but I guess you can say we take particular pleasure in beating Peter."
   Arnold Palmer

Tenth Hole: Hall of Shame Par 5

Hole: 10th Mount Juliet
Par 5 548 yds
Designer: Jack Nicklaus

WEDNESDAY – THE BLOODY PRO-AM

The amateur faces the pro-am with a mixture of anticipatory pride, abject terror, and fretful hope. The professional, more often than not, faces the assignment with resignation. The amateur usually succeeds in living up to his, and the pro's expectations, by playing like a traffic bollard and ruining whatever chance the pro had of becoming better acquainted with the course. Given that two-thirds of all amateur golfers are (statistically) incapable of breaking 90 why do we inflict ourselves on the elite exponents of the game? So that we can brag, that's why. Tell all our loathing mates about "getting a read on that tricky putt from Nick" (unlikely) or "nearly wetting myself when Feherty told another one of his Nicklaus jokes" (more probable).

Doug Sanders tells the story of being teamed with an amateur who was wild off the tee. On about the second hole he was searching for his ball in deep junngle when he bumped into a friend who asked him what pro he was playing with. The response was "I don't know. I haven't met him yet."

Most participants in pro-ams are guests of the corporate sponsors of the tournament, Captains of Industry, Masters of the Universe, busy men – far too busy to play, let alone practise, golf. Hence some of the reactions below of the professionals to these events. I must confess to, at the time of writing, only ever having played in one. It was the 1993 Carrolls Irish Open Pro-Am at Mount Juliet. The delightful Brian Barnes was the pro. Our team failed to electrify. After 31 years Carrolls pulled out of sponsoring the event. I like to think it was just a coincidence.

HACKERS

"The life of the golfer is not all gloom, there's always the lies in the locker room."
From the lyrics of Straight down the Middle *by Sammy Cahn and Jimmy van Heusen*

"The biggest liar in the world is the golfer who says he plays the game merely for exercise."
Tommy Bolt

"There are two things not long for this world – dogs that chase cars and golfers who chip for pars."
Lee Trevino

"The average golfer doesn't play golf. He attacks it."
Jackie Burke

"Golf and sex are the only two things you can enjoy without being good at it."
Jimmy Demaret

"Where Nicklaus will only swing in earnest, not counting the thirty-odd putts of a round, about thirty-four or five times, if not less, a really bad golfer can get in over a hundred strokes, and a few more, possibly, which he won't count."
George Plimpton, who makes it sound like fun

"Big league baseball players are the worst . . . They swing with power, don't ask for advice, and invariably hit to all fields."
Tommy Bolt

"For most amateurs the best wood in the bag is the pencil."
Chi Chi Rodriguez

"Nothing goes down slower than a golf handicap."
Bobby Nichols

"A commanding lead for him would have been two up with one to play."
PG Wodehouse on "Archibald Mealing" in "Archibald's Benefit"

"I played with an amateur in a pro-am once who made eight straight 8s. At the 9th he 3-putted from seven feet for a 9. His caddy looked at him and said, 'Sir, if you had made that putt you'd have made nine straight 8s.' The man just looked at the caddy and said, 'What do you think I am, a machine?'"

Chi Chi Rodriguez

"You could say that it's better than being in Oxford Street, or lying in a hospital bed, or being on remand for several years without trial."

A member of Northwood GC on the joys of the game (from the Channel 4 "Cutting Edge" programme)

"You were hitting some shots out there that weren't making any noise."

Dave Marr to George Plimpton

"Real golfers jump out of the car, change shoes in the car park with one foot on the bumper, then scurry to the tee, take a single practice swipe and lurch into the ball. Then, if their shoulder is still in its socket, they clump off round the course, attempting to shake off last night's hangover and lack of sleep."

Tom O'Connor

"As a broad general rule, the Scots and the Irish tend to nourish handicaps which are higher than their levels of skill; the English tend to brag about handicaps of single figures while being unable to break 90."

Peter Dobereiner

CHEATS

"The score a player reports on a hole should always be regarded as his opening offer."

Henry Beard in "Mulligan's Laws"

"A stroke does not occur unless it is observed by more than one golfer."

Henry Beard in "Mulligan's Laws"

"A ball in the pocket is worth two strokes in the bush."
  Henry Beard in "Mulligan's Laws"

"The basic honesty that prevails in golf is one reason so many are attracted to the game."
  Jimmy Demaret

"One of the troubles with a very high handicap is that the owner is either looked upon as a poor golfer or a possible cheat."
  George Plimpton

"You know the old rule: He who have the fastest cart never had to play bad lie."
  Mickey Mantle, baseball player

"You especially want to make an impression on the lady scorer so she can cheat for you and help you have better statistics in the Greens-in-Regulation and Driving-Distance categories."
  Peter Jacobsen on why he likes to be at the first tee early

"Golf is the hardest game in the world to play and the easiest to cheat at."
  Dave Hill

"I once played at a course where the club cheat is the head of a Fortune 500 corporation."
  Journalist Peter Andrews

"Another thing to remember is that while the ethics of golf forbid coughing, talking, sneezing, snoring or making any other sort of noise while the opponent addresses the ball, it is not illegal to use mustard gas or throw flares or tickle his ears with a wisp of straw."
  Ring Lardner on a possible loophole in the Rules of Golf

"When the Chairman happens to be a short hitter all those sand traps out by the 200-yard marker are suddenly condemned as unfit for human habitation, filled in and turfed over. Show me, as the old saying goes, the Greens Committee Chairman who hasn't chopped at least five strokes off his score, and I'll show you a very angry man."
  Herbert Warren Wind

"Golf is a game in which you yell 'fore', shoot six and write down five."

Paul Harvey

"It's hard to keep score like I do with someone looking over your shoulder."

Bob Hope

"In African countries, too, you are liable to be surrounded by would-be caddies, and here the test is simple. You choose the one with the biggest big toe."

Henry Longhurst

"(They are) in and out of Wormwood Scrubs all the time. They find it hardly worthwhile to get their hair cut in their brief intervals of liberty!"

PG Wodehouse on golfing "cheats"

"I'd like to read you Bernard Cribbins score card, it begins 'Once upon a time'."

Tom O'Connor doing MC at a celeb-am won by the comedian Bernard Cribbins

"Drugs are very much on the scene in professional sports today, but when you think about it, golf is the only sport where the players aren't penalised for being on grass."

Bob Hope

"I never kick my ball in the rough or improve my lie in a sand trap. For that I have a caddy."

Bob Hope

PRO-AMS

"The conspiratorial whisper that every putt breaks towards the sea/lake/mountain/clubhouse, or just whatever major feature happens to dominate the landscape in that particular area. This hole always plays longer/shorter than it looks."

Irish pro and broadcaster David Jones on the endless advice he gets from amateurs in pro-ams

"I play off 18 and a guy who's off 17 starts telling me how to pronate my wrists, and how to address the ball, and whether I'm getting through it fast enough. That tends to piss me off."

Peter Cook, veteran pro-am player

"If that's feathering I'd hate for you to pluck my chickens."

Lee Trevino after his amateur partner insisted that he was going to "feather" an iron

"Tennis players don't have to play in pro-ams. Can you imagine what John McEnroe and Ivan Lendl would say if they were asked to play a quick five-setter with a few of the guys from the local club the day before Wimbledon?"

David Feherty

"Some players are famous for not talking to you. I can't mention names, but his initials are Nick Faldo."

Actor Kevin Whately (Sgt Lewis in "Inspector Morse")

"I've been hit three times in the back and once on the elbow from 30 yards away – with a driver. And the guy laughed. He thought it was funny and my arm had gone numb. That's the closest I've ever come to burying a sand iron in the head of one of the amateurs."

Tony Johnstone

"Anyone can read a putt. It's not hard. Anybody can tell if a painting's crooked on the wall. Well it's not that different from that."

PGA player Mike Clayton on helping amateurs read putts

CELEBRITIES

"What a foolish thing for her to do. Now she'll have to play all her drives off the back tees."

Bing Crosby on hearing of someone who'd had a sex change

"Unfortunately Jack ended up playing the role of an anchor rather than a Kite."

Golf coach Chuck Hogan on Jack Lemmon's latest failed attempt to make the cut at the AT&T National Pro-Am

"Yer know for an old geezer you don't half give it a fucking whack."
The scatological Aussie Wayne Riley to 6-handicapper Christopher Lee

"You don't go home and talk about the great tennis courts that you played but you do talk about the golf courses you played."
Hank Ketcham, creator of "Dennis the Menace"

"With a name like Mary Jones you can get by without stirring up much attention."
The daughter of Bobby Jones on how she avoids being overshadowed by her famous parent

"Bob Hope invented the non-body turn, the interlocking grip on a money clip, the fast backswing and a good short game – off the tee."
Bing Crosby

"My best score ever is 103, but I've only been playing 15 years."
Alex Karras, American Football Hall of Famer

"I can't hit a ball more than 200 yards. I have no butt. You need a butt if you're going to hit a golf ball."
Actor Dennis Quaid after losing two stone to play Wyatt Earp

"For instance, this hole here is a par 47 and you know what? Yesterday I birdied the sucker."
Willie Nelson showing someone around his newly-acquired golf course and maintaining that he could set whatever par he wanted for each hole

"This guy has been in more bunkers than Eva Braun."
Comedian Phil Harris on Jack Lemmon

"When he gets into a tough place, that's when he's most relaxed. I think it's because he has so much experience at it."
Jack Lemmon's caddy

"How could a guy who won the West, recaptured Bataan and won the battle of Iwo Jima let himself be defeated by a little hole in the ground."
Screenwriter James Edward Grant on John Wayne giving up golf

"Bob's got a great short game. Unfortunately it's off the tee."
Jimmy Demaret on Bob Hope

"Jackie's such a generous man that he donated a sweater to charity as a pro-am prize and now there's a family of refugees living in it."
Bob Hope on Jackie Gleason

"Pretty hard to beat a guy who gets a ball out of a sand trap just by muttering a few words and looking up."
Bob Hope on Billy Graham

"Because of the cumbersome suit I was wearing, I couldn't make a very good pivot on the swing. And I had to hit the ball with just one hand."
Alan Shepard, astronaut, on the first golf shot hit on the surface of the moon

"I said a few unprintable words under my breath and called it a Mulligan."
Shepard on flunking his 6-iron shot on the moon

"Ten-nine-eight-seven-six-five-four-three-two-one."
Crowd at Gleneagles celebrity event counting down Shepard as he prepared to hack out of a bunker

"I think I've got the idea now."
Hoagy Carmichael after a hole-in-one

"It took me 17 years to get 3,000 hits in baseball. I did it in one afternoon on the golf course."
Baseball great Hank Aaron

"There's more tension in golf than in boxing because golfers bring it on themselves. It's silly really because it's not as if the golf ball is going to jump up and belt you on the whiskers. Is it?"
Boxer Henry Cooper

"My handicap is that I am a one-eyed Negro."
Sammy Davis Junior

"If I put the ball where I can see it, I can't reach it. If I put it where I can reach it, I can't see it."
The rotund comedian Jackie Gleason

POLITICS

"President Eisenhower has given up golf for painting – it takes fewer strokes."
Bob Hope

"A lot more people beat me now."
Eisenhower on being asked how his game had changed since leaving the White House

"No administration ever had more sun-tanned Secret Service men. You could always find his farm at Gettysburg because it was the one completely surrounded by divots. Ike's neighbours didn't know he'd moved in until Mamie knocked at their door and asked to borrow a cup of golf balls."
Bob Hope

"Not a chance. You run the country, we'll run Augusta."
Augusta Chairman Clifford Roberts to President Eisenhower who asked him might it be possible to remove the tree, now known as "Ike's tree" on the 17th

"During his White House years there was a rumour going around that the new dollar bill would have Ben Hogan's picture on it."
Bob Hope on Eisenhower

"Gerry Ford has made golf a contact sport."
Bob Hope

"I know I'm getting better at golf because I'm hitting fewer spectators."
Former US President Gerald Ford in 1984

"It's a funny thing, Bob. I've just lent Bolivia millions of dollars, but I only have one buck on me to pay you with."
Ford after losing a match to Hope

"I'm either going to throw this up on the green or throw up, depending on the shot."
Former US President George Bush

"It is only appropriate that a Member of Parliament whose constituency borders upon Liverpool and Merseyside should be asked to get up on his hind legs and propose the toast of Cotton."
Lord Brabazon proposing the toast to the Open Champion

"Like throwing darts at a Rembrandt."
Brabazon's reaction to the news that Prince's, Sandwich, was being used as a target range during the war

"An Irish Secretary known to fame
Golfour, links-eyed pursues his favourite game."
Couplet on Arthur "Bloody" Balfour, much reviled Irish Chief Secretary and keen golfer

"He employed two caddies, one for carrying the clubs and the other to act as forecaddie, both being trusted (and fully armed) members of the famous 'G' Division of the DMP."
Article in the Irish Field *on Balfour and his (very necessary) golfing bodyguards*

"I got some hostile letters, none of them giving an address, so I could not write back to the cowards, and the freak fringe of the anti-apartheid brigade had a go at me. One bloke threatened that he was going to chop my arm off."
Woosnam on the reaction to his decision to play in the Sun City Challenge in South Africa in 1988

"The last time I played a round with Vice-President Agnew he hit a birdie, an eagle, a Moose, an Elk and a Mason.
Bob Hope

"At least he can't cheat on his score – because all you have to do is look back down the fairway and count the wounded."
Bob Hope, on Agnew again

"I was his partner one day at Palm Springs, although I didn't realise it until my caddie handed me a blindfold and a cigarette."
Bob Hope on Agnew

"One lesson you'd better learn if you want to be in politics is that you never go out on the golf course and beat the President."

Lyndon Johnson, the late US President

"The difference between golf and government is that in golf you can't improve your lie."

Governor George Deukmejian of California

"Let me get this, Dan, you're unemployed now."

Mark O'Meara after he and former US Vice-President Dan Quayle were due to fork out to a pair of low handicappers to whom they'd lost

Eleventh Hole: Links Par 4

Hole: 11th Ballybunion (Old)
Par 4 449 yds
Designer: Lionel Hewson & others

"Ye do ken ye hae ta clear the burn?" asked the ageing Scottish Caddy, lack of concern etched on his gnarled and wizened features.

"Whassat? Whadya say?" inquired the Tourist anxiously, squinting at the Caddy as he hitched up his blue and grey check trousers before venturing into the knee-deep rough.

"The burn, man, ye hae ta carry it."

The Tourist slashed viciously at the ball through an acre of adolescent hay. Miraculously the white orb emerged from the dense verdant pasture, cleared the browner herbage adjacent to the fairway and headed in the general direction of the green.

The Tourist grinned exultantly at the Caddy, but Methuselah was already a good 50 yards down the fairway.

"Starting to get the hang of this links stuff," he said to himself, loath to be deprived of his small moment of triumph. As he strode after the Caddy he noticed a dark elongated shape snaking its way from the right to the left-hand rough. Goddammit, he thought to himself . . . if that's what I think it is . . . !

It was! His ball, like a dimpled iceberg, was nine-tenths submerged in an eloquently babbling brook.

"Jesus," he berated the Caddy. "Why the hell didn't you tell me there was a stream right across the fairway?"

"Didnae I warn ye?" the Caddy remonstrated, "mak sure tae carry the burn."

"Burn . . . burn . . . what kind of a country is this? This is water . . . you ken? The stuff you guys don't put enough of into your whisky. It's a stream, a waterway, a rivulet, a brook, a lateral water hazard . . . what the hell is a burn?"

The Tourist eyed the offending H_2O as you would a mugger who has just waylaid you at the night safe.

"Tell me something," he inquired, after a few calming deep breaths. "There's plenty of water here, how come you guys don't use it on the fairways?"

It was the Caddy's turn to bristle. He raised a talon, which had once been his right hand and drew an arc in the air which took in the coastal panorama behind the Tourist.

"Yonder's yer watter, mon. Iffen ye want it gae fer a swim."

"Jesus all I'm looking for is some grass that looks green . . . especially on the greens. This is the birthplace of golf, right? How come they ever got round to calling them greens in the first place, why didn't they call 'em what they are, goddamn BROWNS. Those babies take a balata from a 62-degree wedge like a vegetarian takes a steak sandwich."

The Caddy eyed him haughtily. "Ah've seen yer . . . so-called courses . . . on the TV. Ye might as well stick a bullseye where the flag is and go at them with a bow and arrow. Ye're an atheist . . . nae welcome in Nature's Cathedral."

"Nature's . . . Hey, didn't PG Wodehouse say that?"

"He did aye. After he stole it from me. Will ye be takin' a drop?"

The Tourist eyed the Caddy for a moment. Slowly he bent down and began to unlace his shoes. As he did so he said "Hand me that club . . . what did you call it again . . . ?"

"The Mashie-Niblick!"

As he started his backswing, the Tourist, out of the corner of his eye, thought he detected a hint of a satisfied smile on the Caddy's furrowed face.

IRELAND

BALLYBUNION

"When the wind blows, anyone who breaks 70 here is playing better than he is able to play."
Christy O'Connor Sr

" . . . very simply, Ballybunion revealed itself to be nothing less than the finest seaside course I have ever seen."
Herbert Warren Wind

"Ballybunion is a course on which many golf architects should live and play before they build golf courses. I consider it a true test of golf."
Tom Watson

"New Ballybunion is nothing less than the finest links course on earth."
Peter Dobereiner on the New Course at Ballybunion

"This is the most natural golf course terrain I have encountered . . . I will build you a great course, one of my best."
Robert Trent Jones on the New Course, which he designed

COUNTY SLIGO (Rosses Point)

"I went to play one round – and stayed two weeks."
Bernhard Langer

"When the winds blow the only hiding place is to be found back in the clubhouse."
Cecil Ewing

DELGANY

"The nearest thing you can get to a perpendicular golf course. You really need suckers rather than spikes on your shoes as you struggle vertically upwards and then play the next hole back down this precipitous gradient."
Peter Dobereiner

KILDARE HOTEL AND COUNTRY CLUB (The K Club)

"The K Club leaves the visitor wanting nothing, except perhaps an extension to their overdraft facility."
Journalist Daniel Davies

"Looks great. Has Arnold seen it yet?"
Reported comment of Jack Nicklaus flying over the Palmer-designed K Club before it opened

"Instead of one signature hole Palmer leaves his mark with a host of potential card wreckers which look as though they have been beamed straight from the US majors."
Daniel Davies

KILLARNEY

"Pick that up, have the clubs destroyed, and leave the course."
Lord Castlerosse, patron of Killarney Golf Club, to his caddy

"See what the Almighty can do when he is in a good mood."
Unattributed quote on Killarney and its golf courses

"The 18th hole that still adorns the Mahony's Point Course . . . has one almost aching to reach it for the previous 17."
Charlie Mulqueen of the Cork Examiner

"What a lovely place to die."
Henry Longhurst

LAHINCH

"It's OK because I always carry his bag when he's over here and Bob here caddies for me when I'm in New York."
Unidentified (and possibly unemployed) Lahinch caddy to a Department of Social Welfare investigator during a surprise raid

"Lahinch is the St Andrews of Irish golf."
Unattributed but often heard quote

"Dan never did a day's good since he ate mate on Good Friday with the golfers."
Wife of Dan Slattery on whose land Lahinch was constructed

"Sure I'd give you the second but you mightn't have the grass for him."
Maurice de Lacy Staunton giving a half crown tip to a caddy (The half crown featured the emblem of a horse)

"I was so tense I could hear the bees farting."
Mick O'Loughlin, Lahinch golfer, after a putt on the 17th in a South of Ireland semi-final

MOUNT JULIET

"Mount Juliet has set a standard that other courses should follow. I'm delighted that European golf has such a course on its schedule and all our players are certain to benefit from the experience of playing it."
Nick Faldo

PORTMARNOCK

"A private place where a man is alone with the turf, the sea, the sky and the challenge of the wind. It is brave splendid golfing country."
Pat Ward-Thomas

"One of the best little par 4's in golf."
Ben Crenshaw's comment on the par 3 15th

ROYAL COUNTY DOWN

"The finest consecutive holes of links golf."
The judgement of Tom Watson on the first 11 holes

"The view from the hill, over which the golfer drives from the 9th tee, must be as wonderful as any to be had on any course in the British Isles."
Frank Pennink, golf writer

ROYAL PORTRUSH

"Spectacular, breathtaking but also architecturally sound and subtle."
Frank Pennink

TRALEE

"Robert Louis Stevenson got it wrong when he described the Monterey Peninsula as the finest conjunction of land and sea this earth has to offer. As a spectacle, Tralee is in a different class."
Peter Dobereiner

"There are those in the business who say that Palmer couldn't build a bonfire even if you gave him the sticks to do it, but he has done a worthy job here."

Journalist Jock Howard

WATERVILLE

"The beautiful monster – one of the golfing wonders of the world."

Sam Snead

"One of the greatest golf courses ever built."

Henry Cotton

"The most heavenly hell in the world of golf."

Promotional brochure for Waterville

"The courses I play in the States are for pussycats; that one out there is for tigers and hell, I'm no tiger."

TV star Telly Savalas ("Kojak")

"When the west wind comes barrelling in from the Atlantic and the crashing breakers throw mighty plumes of spray high into the air, you feel like King Lear as you brace yourself against the elemental forces on the first tee."

Peter Dobereiner

BRITAIN

CARNOUSTIE

"There are several long ditches or trenches in the rough . . . They're about three-feet deep, and I'm surprised there aren't a lot more one-legged golfers over there because of those ditches."

Ben Hogan on Carnoustie

"The elephants' burial ground."

Johnny Miller on the 1st at Carnoustie (on account of the number of mounds on the fairway)

"Their championship tees are called 'tiger' tees. I thought this was because they were so far back in the heather and gorse that only tigers would be there."

Ben Hogan (The tees for ordinary mortals are called "Rabbits")

"A good swamp spoiled."
Gary Player

MUIRFIELD

"There isn't one poor hole on the course."
Tom Watson on Muirfield

"I don't know why it's regarded as a great golf course; it's certainly not one of my favourites."
Peter Jacobsen

"I don't really want first prize, I just want the hay concession."
Doug Sanders on the Muirfield rough during the 1966 Open

"Young man, this is no public playground. The Open is over."
The fearsome Captain "Paddy" Hanmer, Muirfield secretary, to Open winner Tom Watson (1980) who was playing a game, using hickory-shafted clubs, with Ben Crenshaw

"Are you waiting for inspiration or have you suddenly been taken ill?"
Hanmer shouting at a member who he deemed guilty of slow play

"Muirfield is known, among golf insiders, as the rudest golf club in the world."
Journalist Peter Andrews

"In that event you should come here more often, then I would recognise you."
Former Muirfield Secretary Brian Evans-Lombe after addressing someone he took to be a guest, but who was a member of 20 years standing

PRESTWICK

You would like to gather up several holes from Prestwick and mail them to your top ten enemies."
Dan Jenkins

ROYAL ST GEORGES, SANDWICH

"Fly from Heathrow to Paris, take the train to Calais, hovercraft to Ramsgate then walk down the beach."
Denis Thatcher on the best way to beat the traffic to Royal St Georges during Open week

ST ANDREWS, OLD COURSE

"It is to the golfer what the Vatican is to the Catholic, what Munich is to the beer drinker and what Mount Everest is to the climber."
Hubert Mizell

"If I was set down to play on one course for the rest of my life, I should choose the Old Course at St Andrews."
Bobby Jones

"I could take everything out of my life except my experiences at St Andrews and I'd still have a rich full life."
Bobby Jones on his last visit to the Old Course

"The more you play it, the more you get to know it, the more you respect it."
Jack Nicklaus

"Hey, that looks to me like an old abandoned golf course. What did they call it?"
Sam Snead on seeing the Old Course at St Andrews for the first time, in 1946. He went on to win the Open on the same "abandoned" golf course.

"Until you play it St Andrews looks like the sort of real estate you couldn't give away."
Snead's subsequent judgement

"The only place over there that's holier than St Andrews is Westminster Abbey."
Snead again

"The crowd did give me a bit of stick but that's OK, I've done it before and I'll do it again."
Mark Calcavecchia who took divots with a sand wedge on some of the course's enormous double greens

"The Old Course has a way of making you wish you had stuck to horseshoes."
Charles Price

"An inglorious little thing . . . a paltry little streamlet."
Bernard Darwin on Swilcan Burn, the stream which runs through St Andrews

"Just small enough for an angry man and his sand iron."
A complaint about the Sutherland Bunker which traps shots on the 4th and 15th at St Andrews

"I don't know if you have ever played St Andrews in the wind but it has been known to make scratch players switch to tennis."
Charles Price

"I love the hole, it's an honour to say that I've been eaten alive by it."
Peter Jacobsen on the 17th, the famous Road Hole

"You walk onto the tee praying you're not going to make 10."
Ronan Rafferty on the 17th

"I should have played the hole in an ambulance."
Palmer – after taking 10 on the 17th

ST MELION

"A piece of America in the heart of Cornwall."
Journalist Colin Callender on St Melion, the controversial Nicklaus course

"I always thought Chris Moody was a bit of a prat, but I've changed my mind. He's obviously quite sensible. He didn't come here this week."

Pro Glenn Ralph complaining about the course during the Benson and Hedges tournament

"Arctic conditions prevailed and we all wore so much clothing it was impossible to spot Russell Claydon on the practice ground."

Mark Roe on the 1991 Benson and Hedges at St Melion

"The course is like childbirth, a very painful experience."

David Feherty on St Melion

"I've had enough of this fucking course."

Anders Forsbrand (The course is nicknamed St Smelly One by the tour pros)

"I think the owners were conned. I think that one was designed by Jack's wife, Barbara."

David Feherty (Later he regretted that comment – because of the implied insult to Barbara Nicklaus)

USA

AUGUSTA

"When I walked out on the grass terrace under the big trees behind the house and looked down over the property, the experience was unforgettable. It seemed that this land had been lying here for years just waiting for someone to lay a golf course upon it."

Bobby Jones on his first sight of the property which became Augusta National

"It is the most beautiful of all golf gatherings. It is a pageant in the pines."

Robert Trent Jones on Augusta

"I have always said that if they have a golf course like this in Heaven, I want to be the head pro."

Gary Player on Augusta National

"Augusta . . . reduces putting to something between a lottery and a farce."
Gary Player

"Gathering breakneck speed with every turn, the ball ran straight into the centre of the cup. 'Great read, sir' beamed Douglas (the caddy) surreptitiously slipping the wedge back into the bag."
Irish Times *Golf Correspondent, Dermot Gilleece, holing a long putt on the 1st and avoiding a pitch back from off the same green*

"Not necessarily, it simply requires more skill than I possess at the moment."
Ben Hogan on being asked was the 12th at Augusta "impossible"

"It was the last time anyone saw Weiskopf with hair."
Unattributed comment after Tom Weiskopf's 13 at the 12th in the 1980 Masters. The following day he took a 7.

"The meanest little hole in the world."
Lloyd Mangrum on the 12th hole

"The most demanding tournament hole in golf."
Jack Nicklaus on the 12th

"I hope I don't have to play that hole again. Next year I think I'll lay up short."
Dan Forsman on dumping his ball into the water in front of the 12th hole in the middle of Amen Corner when challenging during the last round of the 1993 Masters

CYPRESS POINT

"The wind always howls, usually dead in your face and rumour has it the seals down on the rocks below raise one flipper to call for a fair catch on all the balls dropping over the cliff."
Peter Jacobsen on the 16th, where the tee and green are on opposite sides of a cove

"It's . . . very exclusive. Cypress had a very successful membership drive last month. They drove out 40 members."
Bob Hope

"Frostily exclusive but staggeringly beautiful."
Broadcaster Cliff Michelmore

HAZELTINE

"All it needed was some cows and a few acres of corn to be a perfect farm."
Dave Hill after the US Open in 1970 won by Tony Jacklin

"You can't change the golf course. I have always tried to take the view that you woo the golf course and try to make friends with it rather than criticise it."
Jacklin on the much criticised Hazeltine course

MUIRFIELD VILLAGE

"It's a pretty little jewel until it eats your lunch once or twice. Then, like the prom queen who loses her dentures when she bites into a cheeseburger, she never looks quite the same again."
Peter Jacobsen on the par 3, 12th

OAKMONT

"You had to manipulate the ball into the hole, not putt it."
Tommy Armour after winning the 1927 US Open at Oakmont

"I've played Oakmont. A photographer kept shooting me every time I swung. I was very flattered until I found out he was from *Field and Stream*."
Bob Hope

PEBBLE BEACH

"It was Alcatraz with grass. There were wind and rain, rocks and shrubs and trees and animals, and that was on the greens. I've heard of unplayable lies, but on the tee . . . ?
Bob Hope

"They've had rain so many times they're thinking of holding tournaments indoors. I've often wondered what it was like to play golf inside a ball washer."

Bob Hope

"I've seen better courses. Number 7, I thought it was a practice hole, and there are too many blind shots."

Ian Woosnam, in 1992, on the celebrated par 3 seventh

"He said that about this course. I can't believe it."

Paul Azinger on Woosnam

"Well, that's his opinion. Actually, he's right about number seven if there's no wind."

Tom Watson on Woosnam

"Playing Pebble Beach is like fighting Rocky Marciano. Every time you step onto the course, you're a cinch to take a beating."

Jack Burke

"For those who believe that man came from the sea and faces a deep hidden necessity to return to it some day, there would be no better route than to get a golf club and go to the 18th at Pebble Beach."

Dan Jenkins

PINE VALLEY

"Foursomes have left the first tee there and have never been seen again. They just find their shoelaces and bags."

Bob Hope

"I once did this hole in 2. For several days life had nothing more to offer."

Henry Longurst on the 5th at Pine Valley

"An examination in golf."

Bernard Darwin

"It is all very well to punish a bad stroke, but the right of eternal punishment should be reserved for a higher tribunal than a Greens Committee."

Bernard Darwin after going level par for the first seven holes then taking a 16 at the short 8th

"Only God can make three."

Unattributed reference to the par 3 fifth

"One must play Pine Valley the way a porcupine courts its mate, very carefully."

Journalist Cal Brown

SAWGRASS, TPC

Journalist: "What's the difference between the Player's Championship and the British Open?"
Lyle: "About 120 years."

Sandy Lyle getting The Player's Championship in perspective as "the fifth Major"

EAST OF THE CHANNEL TUNNEL

"It wasn't so bad that you would have awarded three golf balls for the spectator nearest to the 18th green, but it wasn't far off it."

Peter Alliss on the lack of crowds at some European tour venues

"There are more out of bounds than Alcatraz."

Christy O'Connor Jr on the Golf de Guadiana course in Spain

"Not so much a golf course as a penal colony. It's where the Royal Marines would take a golf holiday. We're talking Elba Country Club."

Journalist Richard Stafford on Parque de Floresta in Portugal

"It was the last act committed by Walt Disney before he died."

David Feherty on Valderrama

"C'est magnifique, mais ce n'est pas le golf."

Henry Longhurst's reflection on Masjid-i-Sulaiman Golf Club in Iran

"It's a real good course, but walking from the greens to the next tee is like playing nine extra holes."

Gardner Dickinson on the Sohbu Country Club in Japan

"I wish we could roll these fairways up and take them along with us."

Bruce Crampton on Sohbu

"It soaks through and improves the fairways."

Unattributed comment on the Royal Benghazi GC which is often under the sea

"They have nine greens, no tees and one flag, which is brought out each time anyone wishes to play. No good having regular flags, since, if they were made of wood, the ants would eat them and, if of metal, they would be instantly melted down by the locals for spears."

Henry Longhurst on the El Fasher GC in Sudan

Twelfth Hole: Swing Thoughts Par 4

Hole: 12th Tralee
Par 4 448 yds
Designer: Arnold Palmer & Ed Seay

"Life is not backswing, it is all follow through." The first pearls of wisdom I ever heard from my personal guru Ka Zwell Wattah, the Eastern mystic. A man who had never ever seen a golf club in his life but whose holistic approach to existence touched directly on golf as a wheel does on the gravel beneath it.

A room piled high with videos, magazines, instructional books, the corpses of teaching professionals who had failed to bring lower scores – this was my monument to futility. My Wax Museum. But then, a whisper in the trees, like something out of a Kevin Costner movie. "If you call him – toll free – he will come." It was worth every penny fetched by the family home and the sale of wife and kids into white slavery in Morocco.

"Uncloud your mind, unclog your senses, feel the force grip you from within, breathe in the wind of a thousand dreams . . . and don't forget to pronate your wrists." He said, as he searched my wallet for American Express. Under his caring guidance my game flowered, prospered, bloomed, grew. My scoring was worse than ever but he made me see how unimportant that was. How vulgar and petty it was to dig in the fetid dirt of competition. I learned to be at peace never breaking 120.

With my money finally gone, as he, with profound regret kicked me out of the ashram in Lakenonaflorida I begged him for one last defining moment. For one final revelation. What was the essence of his mission? Why was he here? He looked at me dubiously for a moment, then, relenting, he removed the hand of the lissom ingénue stroking his thigh and replied. "It is the Intent of every HOLY MAN (He often spoke in upper case) merely to pass on what he has come to know, merely to LEAD BETTER." Hallelujah!

LEARNING AND PRACTICE

"It breeds great perfection if the practice be more difficult than the play."
Elizabethan scientist and philosopher Francis Bacon (So what if he wasn't talking about golf – quotes like this give a chapter just the right air of pretentiousness!)

"What a shame to waste those great shots on the practice tee."
Walter Hagen on why he never bothered

"That is nothing but corporal punishment."
Hagen watching players practice

"No one who ever had lessons would have a swing like mine."
Lee Trevino

"If you're not prepared, somewhere in the quiz there are going to be some questions you can't answer."
Charles Coody

"Can't you just let one of them go in. I mean, it is the practice green."
Simon Hobday talking to the heavens after lipping out three times in succession on the practice green

"Give me a millionaire with a bad backswing and I can have a very pleasant afternoon."
George Low

"What do you mean? My weight is where it is, I can't order it about."
William Haley, editor of The Times, *when told how to distribute his weight during his first lesson*

"If you can't outplay them, outwork them."
Ben Hogan

"Missing a short putt doesn't mean that I have to hit my next drive out of bounds."
Tony Lema

"If I miss one day's practice I know it; if I miss two days' practice the spectators know it, and if I miss three days the world knows it."
   Ben Hogan after the great Polish pianist Paderewski

"There was tape all over my hand and blood all over the tape."
   "Babe" Zaharias, who practised hard

"Whatever do you want to do that for. You know how to play golf already."
   Henry Longhurst to a shocked Gary Player who had just told him he'd hit a thousand practice balls the previous week

"Lessons are not to take the place of practice but to make practice worthwhile."
   Harvey Penick

"Swinging at daisies is like playing electric guitar with a tennis racket; if it were that easy we could all be Jerry Garcia. The ball changes everything."
   Michael Bamberger on the futility of the practice swing (And if you don't know who Jerry Garcia is you're either under 30 or over 50)

"As soon as you start thinking, 'Hey, this is easy, I've got the answer,' somebody changes the question."
   David Feherty on confidence

"The nice thing about these books is that they usually cancel each other out. One book tells you to keep your eye on the ball, the next says not to bother. Personally, in the crowd I play with, a better idea is to keep your eye on your opponent."
   Jim Murray, Los Angeles Times, *on tuition books*

"If some of them tried to bring a fork up to their mouths the way they try to take a club on the backswing, they would starve to death."
   Sam Snead on golfers who get bogged down by theory

"Practice golf . . . is like a boxer working on a punch bag. It doesn't hit back."
   Chi Chi Rodriguez

"Look at those guys wasting their time practising that long, slow backswing. Me, I'm snatching that club up and down like we'll all be doing tomorrow when the tournament starts."

Al Watrous watching competitors practising for a tournament

TEACHING

"As far as swing and techniques are concerned, I don't know diddley squat. When I'm playing well, I don't even take aim."

Fred Couples at a golf clinic

"When I ask you to take an aspirin, please don't take the entire bottle. In the golf swing a tiny change can make a huge difference."

Harvey Penick

"George, show this gentleman a proper set of clubs."

One-time Coombe Hill pro Archie Compston to his clubmaker. A regular gambit to show the pupils who was boss.

"The secret he had shown me in the morning never worked in the afternoon, but he always discovered a new one on the 17th hole and went home happy and with something to show me the next morning."

Bobby Jones on his father

"I've seen golf books . . . which were as difficult to read as advanced textbooks in physics, which, in fact they somewhat resembled."

Arnold Palmer

"You know that a line, in mathematics, is in fact a series of points? Most people see only the line, but the mathematician can see the points. That's what happened with the golf swing. We teachers became mathematicians, seeing all these bloody points, but we lost track of the line."

Scottish pro John Stark talking to Michael Bamberger

"It's not the player who knows where the club should be who is successful it's the player who knows where the club is."

David Feherty

"Y'know it's hard to teach the game. Man's like a narrow-mouthed whiskey bottle. He can only take a word or two at a gulp."
Scottish pro Alec "Nipper" Campbell

"All you got to do to write a book is win one tournament. All of a sudden you're telling everyone where the Vs ought to point."
George Low

"Back . . . Hit."
Timothy Gallwey's mantra for the Inner Game

"This is a driver . . and this is a putter."
Manuel Pinero explaining golf to a Spanish TV audience

"In designing a golf course, you just cut away and move dirt and remove everything that doesn't look like a golf course, and in golf instruction the teacher eventually has to say, 'Enough cutting, now go play.'"
Peter Jacobsen

"Do you know what the worst single sight in golf is? It's a father hovering over his son or daughter as they hit balls on a range. It's sick. How can you expect a child to develop a feel for the game when every movement is analysed and critiqued."
Nick Price on pushy parents

GURUS

"I've never had a swing coach because I never found one who could beat me in a game of golf."
Lee Trevino establishing a dangerous criterion for the new generation of gurus

"I've been working for a long time, trying to draw the ball, and it keeps going right. I used to work with Bob Torrance but I'm on my own now. Why waste money?"
Ian Woosnam on the great Scottish teacher (A few short weeks later he was begging Torrance to come to Augusta and help him before the Masters)

"If human beings did not have a tendency to interfere with their own ability to perform and learn, there would be no Inner Game."
The guru of golf psychologists, Timothy Gallwey

"Dig it out of the dirt, the way I did."
Ben Hogan on being asked for swing advice by another pro

"I can't criticise Nick Faldo for having David Leadbetter beside him at every tournament. The truth is that Nick wasn't a particularly good player before they teamed up. Leadbetter has effectively given him another pair of eyes."
Jack Nicklaus

"As I get older I must be becoming a better teacher. This must be true, because more of my pupils have started hitting the ball out of my sight."
Harvey Penick on fading eyesight

"I've been told that if you take an infant child and drop it into a swimming pool, it will somehow manage to paddle around without drowning. This may be true, but it's a theory I would hate to test. Most people jump into golf the same way."
Jack Grout, teacher to Jack Nicklaus

"David is not going to turn a chop into a player."
Nick Price on David Leadbetter

"I became a better player; a player I could never have been without the teaching methods of David Leadbetter."
Nick Faldo

"They can pay the expenses to bring those fellows to big tournaments, can afford long-distance calls to ask advice. We couldn't do that years ago."
Gary Player on modern players and their gurus

"When you go to the first tee at Augusta National, you've got to leave your Sony in your locker."
Old pro Jackie Burke Jr on the ubiquitous Sony videocam on practice grounds

"If they're such great teachers why can't they take a raw kid of 15 and make him a champion."
Trevino on the modern golf "guru"

"I'm a man of many coats: friend, coach, teacher, psychologist."
David Leadbetter

"You're refining little things, you're pumping them up. Golf isn't a game where you have your team mates to cheer you up. You need your coach."
David Leadbetter

"There are four learning modes, analytical or cognitive, kinasthetic or feel, visual or mime, concrete experience."
Coach Peter Kostis (Thanks Peter!)

"My boy, two things. Always have your clubs with you when you go to play. And take different routes to your bank because someone may be following you."
The only pearls of wisdom proffered by Claude Harmon during a lesson with Lanny Wadkins

"Let them see the good players and they'll imitate. That's the way to learn."
John Jacobs on coaching young players

TIPS AND ADVICE

"To everything there is a season. A time to get and a time to lose. A time to keep and a time to cast away."
Ecclesiastes (Just thought we'd kick off with another pretentious quote)

"If you really want to get better at golf, go back and take it up at a much earlier age."
Henry Beard in "Mulligan's Laws"

"The only shots you can be dead sure of are those you've had already."
Byron Nelson

"The golf swing is like sex in this respect. You can't be thinking about the mechanics of the act while you're performing."
Dave Hill

"Don't be afraid. Fear will influence your muscles, so dismiss fear."
Ben Hogan

"A golfer must always move freely beneath himself."
A tip from the English pro of the inter-war years, Abe Mitchell

"Real golfers never question their client's score."
Unattributed

"Tienes las manos. Ahora juega con tu corazon." ("You have the hands. Now play with your heart.")
The advice of Roberto di Vicenzo to Seve Ballesteros during the 1979 Open

"You've got to learn that the best shot possible is not always the best shot to play."
Amatuer Bill Fownes to Bobby Jones

"Never try to play a shot you haven't practised."
Harvey Penick, golf instructor

"Dance with what brung you!"
Harvey Penick advising against major adjustments during a round

"Why don't you try hitting the ball with your backswing?"
Scottish pro Stewart Maiden's wry advice to Bobby Jones to slow down, after watching him practice for the 1925 US Open

"I do a lot of humming out on the course. I tend to stick with one song . . . I shot a 66 to 'Moon River'."
Jack Nicklaus

"Gary solicits far too much advice on the practice tee – I've seen him taking a lesson at the US Open from a hot-dog vendor."
Dave Hill on Gary Player

"Under an assumed name."

"Dutch" Harrison's response when asked by his amateur partner how he should play a particular shot

"I never leave myself a half shot if I can help it . . . If I leave myself a tricky little half shot and don't hit it just right over that water, that dog ain't gonna hunt."

Lee Trevino

"Lay off for three weeks and then quit for good."

Sam Snead's advice to a hacker

"You've just one problem, you stand too close to the ball – after you've hit it."

Snead's advice to another hacker

"There's an old saying: If a man comes home with sand in his cuffs and cockleburs in his pants, don't ask him what he shot."

Sam Snead

"Keep on hitting it straight until the wee ball goes in the hole."

Sound advice from the great turn-of-the-century pro James Braid

"Isn't it funny how you remember bad advice longer than good advice?"

Tom O'Connor

"Let the nothingness into your shoes."

The fictional pro Shivas Irons, in Michael Murphy's book "Golf in the Kingdom"

Thirteenth Hole: Real Life Par 3

Hole: 13th The Island
Par 3 210 yds
Designer: Fred Hawtree, Eddie Hackett & others

Randall Knapp, journeyman pro, eyed his ball dubiously. It might as well have been in the adjacent cemetery so deeply was it buried. Desperately he looked around for a staked tree so that he could claim some relief. He had spent most of the morning hacking out from behind, under or beside trees of all shapes and sizes. Now, just when he needed the thinnest of saplings the only wood to be found in the vicinity was a discarded lollipop stick.

He was about to give up hope and count his blessings that he had even found the ball when he spotted something yellowish lying just in front of it. On closer inspection it turned out to be the remains of the business end of the lollipop which some young spectator had obviously been given by a distracted father to get the bored child to shut up.

Randall suddenly felt very pleased with himself. His fertile golf brain had shown him the solution to his immediate difficulty. He hailed the PGA official responsible for the hole.

"Casual water," he said triumphantly, pointing to the fast melting iced lollipop. "It's interfering with my shot. I'm claiming a drop."

"You must be joking. That's not casual water . . . that's a bloody lollipop," the PGA official remonstrated.

"Rule 25 'Snow and ice are either casual water or loose impediments, at the option of the player . . . '" Randall began.

"' . . . except that manufactured ice is an obstruction.'" the PGA official continued. "Which means you can simply move the obstruction and get on with it."

"Yes, agreed. But that's not manufactured ice. It's frozen orange juice . . . casual orange juice. So I get a free drop."

By now a crowd had gathered and was listening with concentrated interest. From behind the ropes a booming voice ripped through the reverential stillness.

"Heard what you said . . . you've got a case. Take counsel's opinion. I'm an SC. No charge!"

From just behind the first voice came a second, even louder and more authoritative.

"Counsel's opinion isn't worth a damn. It's just the half-baked surmise of an overpaid, overfed, overwatered fraud. I'm a High Court Judge and I don't agree. Frozen orange juice quite definitely comes under the heading 'manufactured ice', Popsicle Petes vs Lollipop Lils, 1992, *ipso facto*, it's a removable obstruction."

"Not true at all, not true at all." This from a third, much older and more dignified contributor. "I've reversed too many High Court decisions to pay a blind bit of attention to what a jumped-up Circuit Court judge has to say about anything. The Appeal in re Popsicle Petes vs Lollipop Lils overturned the High Court decision, just last week. I know, I wrote the majority decision. He gets his drop."

A discussion between the three men, Knapp and the PGA official followed. As it got more heated nobody noticed a small child creep under the ropes and head towards Knapp's ball. Suddenly he bent down and grabbed what was left of the lollipop. He waved it in the air exultantly, jumped up and down in glee and roared, "Daddy, Daddy, I told you it was here."

Knapp looked on in horror as the child's heel landed on his ball forcing it into the pasture-like grass. But his discomfort didn't last long. His brain clicked into action. He turned animatedly towards the official and spoke, emphasising every syllable.

"Rule 18-1 'If a ball at rest is moved by an outside agency the player shall incur no penalty and the ball shall be replaced before the player plays another stroke.'"

NON-GOLFERS

"There is no room on earth to destroy nature for the sake of a mere game."

General Morita, Japanese environmentalist and founder member of the Global Anti-Golf Movement

"If I had my way, a man guilty of golf would be ineligible for any public office in the United States, and the families of the breed would be shipped off to the white slave corrals of the Argentine."
HL Mencken

"An open exhibition of overweening ambition, courage deflated by stupidity, still scoured by a whiff of arrogance."
Alistair Cooke on golf, before he began playing the game

"Golf is just the old-fashioned pool hall moved outdoors, but with no chairs around the walls."
Will Rogers, American humourist

"Would you like to see a city given over soul and body to a tyrannising game?"
An unidentified American student writing about the university town of St Andrews

"Harvey, that game you play doesn't make sense. You hit a ball 250 yards off the tee and it counts for one stroke, the same as a 3- or 4-foot putt."
Woman to Harvey Penick

"The eye of the Oldest Member was thoughtful and reflective. When it looked into yours you saw in it that perfect peace, that peace beyond understanding, which comes at its maximum only to a man who has given up golf."
PG Wodehouse

"Golf, I'm convinced was conceived by real estate developers so they could have an excuse for tearing up perfectly good forests and pastures."
American humourist Lewis Grizzard

"I'd do better if the ball was two feet off the ground and moving."
Baseballer Stan Musial

"Golf is a nobody's game!"
Baseballer Willie Mays

183

"There is more excitement and spectacle in a competition to decide the world's largest parsnip."
Michael Parkinson

"The environmental correspondent of the *Observer* . . . recently suggested that in the national interest all golf courses should be ploughed up and made into allotments. There can be no arguing with this outstanding piece of common sense. Vegetables are more important than golfers and, aesthetically speaking, I'd rather watch a cabbage grow than a man worrying his guts over a 2-foot putt."
Michael Parkinson

"Why shouldn't he? He's never done anything all his life but play golf."
Joe Turnesa, unimpressed father on being told his son was leading the 1926 US Open

"One of the advantages bowling has over golf is that you seldom lose a bowling ball."
Professional American bowler Don Carter

"Any game where a man aged 60 can beat a man aged 30 ain't no game."
Burt Shotten, baseball manager

"Golf's not that hard. The ball doesn't move!"
Baseball player Ted Williams (Said, presumably, before he actually played the game!)

"The great mystery about the game is why people who play it so abysmally enjoy it so much."
John Naughton, Observer *columnist*

"Why do golfers on the green first knock the ball up to the hole, and then put it in?"
Bernard Darwin, quoting a billiards professional

"Golf is a game whose aim is to hit a very small ball into an even smaller hole with weapons singularly ill-designed for the purpose."
Sir Winston Churchill

"Every time I have the urge to play golf I lie down until the urge passes."

Sam Levenson, American writer

"A non-playing member of a golf club may be defined as one who spends more time at the club than anyone else, but is never seen hitting a ball with a club. Based on the principle that a round of golf is always more enjoyable in retrospect than at the time, his belief is that golf is much more enjoyable when you have totally given up playing."

Miles Kington, on the laws of the non-playing member

"There are now more golf clubs in the world than Gideon bibles, more golf balls than missionaries and, if every golfer in the world, male and female, were laid end to end, I, for one, would leave them there."

Michael Parkinson

"I don't see the point in chasing a little white ball around a field."

Calvin Coolidge, US President

"Fergie apparently expected her husband to be a fun-loving companion; by all accounts, he has become an indifferent couch potato and, worse yet, a golfer."

Newsweek *magazine on the break up of the marriage of the Duke and Duchess of York*

"I think hitting a golf ball is insane because you have to go chase it. But when you lift a weight and put it down, its still there at your feet."

US Olympic weightlifter Rich Schutz

RULES

"I've always had three rules for playing well on the tour: no push-ups, no swimming, and no sex after Wednesday."

Sam Snead

"I do not know the Rules of Golf, I never have known them, and I am too old to begin learning them now. I think it is ridiculous that we cannot hit our little balls round with our little sticks without 93 pages of rules and an ever-increasing volume of case law in the form of Decisions, many of them, so I am assured, contradictory to each other."

Henry Longhurst

"The rules invite cheating. They take up more printed pages than the Constitution of the United States and are less perfectly understood. How can we be expected to follow them. It's like trying to keep up with the tax code."
Journalist Peter Andrews

"Is it against the rules to carry a bulldozer in your bag?"
Tom Watson complaining about the greens at the TPC in Sawgrass

"One, play the ball as it lies. Two, play the course as you find it. Three, when it is not possible to do either, do what's fair."
Tom Watson on the three basic rules of golf

"Every time you leave a loophole in anything, somebody takes advantage of it, contrary to the spirit of the game and another rule has to be brought in to close the gap."
David Jones

"You only get relief from red ants."
Referees remark to Sandy Lyle in a Zambian tournament after Lyle asked for a free drop from a swarm of black ants

"You might as well have praised a man for not robbing a bank."
Bobby Jones surprised at being praised for penalising himself a stroke for an infraction which no one else spotted

"Nobody ever cheats anybody else at golf. The one who is cheated is the one who cheats."
Tommy Armour

"My God, the courses these kids play today are either half casual water or ground under repair . . . One of these days I'm going to write a book on drops. That ought to sell. The shot's become more popular than putting."
Jimmy Demaret

"In competition during or while the bombs are falling, players may take cover without penalty for ceasing to play."
Wartime British rule

"A player whose stroke is affected by the simultaneous explosion of a bomb or shell, or by machine-gun fire, may play another ball from the same place. Penalty, one stroke."

A less lenient British wartime rule

"Here, you try and play it."

Jose Maria Olazabal remonstrating with PGA Tour Tournament Director John Paramor about not getting any relief from a plugged bunker lie (All he got was a £250 fine)

"The ball was 1.62 inches in diameter as compared to 1.68 for the American ball and that meant less wind resistance, fewer dimples on the ball and less spin. To me, playing with the small ball was like cheating."

Lee Trevino

"Golf, in fact, is the only game in the world in which a precise knowledge of the rules can earn a reputation for bad sportsmanship."

Patrick Campbell

"You play the game by the rules, and that in itself is the infallible mark of a gentleman of quality."

Tommy Armour

"Can you imagine the referee telling Steve Davis to get a move on as he approached a 147 break."

Gary Evans, heading for a 66 in the PGA at Wentworth being fined £250 for slow play (Mind you Steve Davis plays under artificial light)

"I think most of the rules of golf stink. They were written by the guys who can't even break 100."

Chi Chi Rodriguez

"The game has been blessed with having men of probity on committees for more than half a century, men who are not financially rewarded in any way for their labours. The game is in good hands."

Peter Alliss on the rulemakers

LIFE, DEATH AND TAXES

"I'm gambling that when we get into the next life, St Peter will look at us and ask, 'Golfer?' And when we nod, he will step aside and say, 'Go right in, you've suffered enough.' One warning, if you do go in and the first thing you see is a par 3 surrounded by water, it ain't Heaven."

Jim Murray

"My kids now call me Yul Brynner or Charlie Brown and, for our family, bald is fun."

Paul Azinger on chemotherapy

"If I had known it would be this easy I wouldn't have worried about it."

Bobby Jones on Death, three days before he died

"There was a thunderous crack like cannon fire and suddenly I was lifted a foot and a half off the ground. Damn, I thought to myself, this is a hell of a penalty for slow play."

Lee Trevino on being struck by lightning in 1975

"We don't want anybody killed. Of course, if we could pick which ones, it might be a different story."

Hord Hardin postponing play at the Masters owing to lightning

"I thought they were making a movie, and I was looking around for the cameras. Then I realised it was for real."

David Feherty on running into a gunfight between two motorists while on a jog in California

"When you play professional golf you lose the ability to play simply for fun. If I'm playing a practice round, and I hit a 2-iron just perfectly, I don't get a buzz. I get nothing. Unless it happens in a tournament, in competition, it doesn't mean a thing."

Peter Teravainen

"Playing golf is not hot work. Cutting sugar cane for a dollar a day – that's hot work. Hotter than my first wrist-watch."

Chi Chi Rodriguez on a rough start in life

"I just hope I live long enough to see my daughter get out of college. After that they can hand me something to drink, I don't care."
Lee Trevino

"We're all trying to steal Nancy's birth-control pills, but so far we've been unsuccessful."
Fellow pro Joanne Carner on Nancy Lopez

"How can you have families who don't even have health insurance, because it's too expensive? If this is such a great country how can that happen? And you have 14-year-old kids going through metal detectors to go to school – I mean, what a sick society."
Swedish US PGA pro, Helen Alfredsson on the USA

"The number of deaths from sundry causes on the golf course is quite extraordinary, ranging from the father who was instructing his son and was killed by a practice swing, to the man who broke his shaft against a tree and cut his throat with the dismembered half."
Henry Longhurst

"If I died . . . it meant I couldn't play golf. No way was I giving up golf, so I gave up drinking."
Bob Hope

"I have given my wife a power of attorney so that, if the time comes when I can no longer play golf, she is to send for the vet and have me put down."
Told to Henry Longhurst in Tripoli

"My handicap? Arthritis."
Bobby Jones at the age of 45

"I've never found sex that exciting, not nearly as exciting as golf."
Dave Hill

"My enthusiasm for the game has dwindled in that I've found something more interesting than golf – a wife."
Bruce Lietzke, the "Invisible Man" of the US PGA Tour

"I've had sex in a lot of places. I wouldn't want to have it in the bunker, because of the sand. I'd kind of like to have it on the green; it would be nice and soft."

Jan Stephenson in a Playboy *interview*

"He folded her in his arms, using the interlocking grip."

PG Wodehouse

"Studying psychology isn't that relevant to the tour. What college really prepares you for is graduate school."

Tom Watson

"That's what happens if you haven't been home in 18 years."

Lee Trevino on the reason for a divorce

"I'm going for broke. I was born broke, so I want to live like a millionaire and die poor; I don't want to live poor and die like a millionaire."

Chi Chi Rodriguez

"There's not as much pressure on the golf tour. Walking to the first tee is in no way comparable to walking through the jungle in combat.

Vietnam veteran and US pro Larry Nelson

"It isn't golf, it's the travelling. I want to die an old man, not a young man."

Hogan, in 1949, cutting back on competition (He had almost been killed in a car crash)

"This much I can tell you for sure, Joe. There's nothing about death that will ever frighten me again."

Ben Hogan to journalist Joe Williams after his near-fatal car crash

"Baseball players quit playing and they take up golf. Basketball players quit, take up golf. Football players quit, take up golf. What are we supposed to take up when we quit."

George Archer on retirement

"Me retire? Retire to what. All I do now is fish and play golf."

Julius Boros, once an accountant, but became a pro golfer at 30

"We're getting too old, Willie and I. I think we had better get a dog to read the greens for us."

Trevino on himself and caddy Willie Aitchison

"I'm working as hard as I can to get my life and my cash to run out at the same time. If I can just die after lunch Tuesday, everything will be fine."

Doug Sanders

"A golf club provides an opportunity for a disappointed man to achieve some kind of prominence."

A member of Northwood GC on the Channel 4 "Cutting Edge" programme

"Now it is time to lay down my pen and, alas, the microphone, too, and to reflect, in whatever time may be left, how uncommonly lucky I have been. And if I have managed to give a little pleasure on the way, well, what a happy thought that is too."

The last written words of Henry Longhurst. He died on 21 July, 1978.

Fourteenth Hole: Mixed Bag Par 4

Hole: 14th Waterville
Par 4 458 yds
Designer: Eddie Hackett & John A Mulcahy

"It's **A**erodynamically efficient."

"**B**alata – that's the **B**all for you, think of the **B**ackspin."

"Go for the 100 **C**ompression, look at your forearms, you can probably **C**rush it."

"**D**esigners? Well, of course I'm used to **D**ye courses."

"**E**quipment? Stick with the pro shop, you don't know what you're getting in the High Street."

"You need a big **F**lange, to get the bounce, d'ye see."

"**G**rooves? I wouldn't get excited. Wait till Ping win in the Supreme Court."

"They eliminate the **H**osel. That's the beauty of these big-headed drivers!"

"The Ping **Eye** 2, your only man, will I gift wrap it for him, ma'am?"

"**J**ust wait till you see the Big Bertha metal-headed sand wedge."

"No, no, you need a club with a low **K**ick point for your type of game."

"Here, try this new wedge with the 85-degree **L**oft."

"**M**etal-headed clubs are on the way out. Here, try this, the new persimmon putter."

"**N**ick Price swears by them, sir."

"It refers to the clubhead, sir. I'm afraid there's no way to **O**ffset the cost of the club."

"These are extra heavy golf shoes. We're trying to introduce the concept of **P**erimeter weighting for players."

"Only a few **Q**uid more, but, trust me, you'll see the difference in your scorecard."

"The **R**oyal and Ancient actually endorse this ball."

"I'm sorry, sir, but you're not actually allowed carry a **S**timpmeter around with you."

"I'll have none of that sort of **T**orque in my shop. Good, wha?"

"**U**mbrella! Why not just hire a buggy, sir?"

"Get those **V**s pointing at the your right shoulder and you'll be well set."

"This particular **W**edge gives you a computer print-out of what goes wrong each time you use it."

"Those broom-handled putters should be **X**-rated. Over 50s only." ·

"**Y**ears, **Y**ears. It should have lasted **Y**ears. Anyway, this is the very latest. Guaranteed . . . "

"**ZZZZZZZZ** . . . Sorry, sir. Did I lose you somewhere?"

BAGGAGE

"No man with funny head-covers ever broke par."
Henry Beard in "Mulligan's Laws"

"Lynx Tigress G – More than ladies cosmetics. Like unsheathing a set of your own claws."
Magazine advertisement

"Spring was designed like an old set of MacGregor irons – to rejuvenate the soul."
Deane Beman US PGA Tour Commissioner

"A club is like an automobile; performance can make it look either ugly or beautiful."
Gary Hallberg, American pro

"Since the first shepherd hit the first stone at a distant mole hole, better ways have been sought for performing such an act."
Robert Trent Jones Sr

"A golf club should be like a work of art, a piece of fine jewellery."
Ben Hogan

"All this fiddling with clubs, taping, altering lies, grips and angles, frankly bores me."
Gary Player

"The last thing I want if I'm under pressure is to not have a friend in my hand."
Nick Price on his golf clubs

"I used to use three a round, but since I bought the company I only use one."
Jack Nicklaus on gloves

"Do not be tempted to invest in a sample of each golfing invention as soon as it makes its appearance. If you do, you will only complicate and spoil your game – and encumber your locker with much useless rubbish."
Harry Vardon

"How are you getting on with your new clubs?" asked the golfer when he walked into the bar and saw a friend of his. "Fine," replied the friend. "They put 20 yards on my slice."
Dai Rees anecdote

"It was like swinging a scaffolding pole."
Ian Pyman, Amateur Medal winner Open Championship 1993, after trying out John Daly's "Killer Whale" driver

"Where'd you get this ugly thing? Man, this is one of them airport drivers. That's right! You hit this thing for two days, miss the cut and go to the airport!"
Lee Trevino examining a competitor's driver

"On the 18th hole, a par 4, I first thought of using my 4-wood on my second shot. But, you see, my 4-wood is actually a 5-wood and my 3-wood is actually a 4-wood. Realising my 4-wood would wind up short – that's actually my 5-wood – I went instead to my 3-wood, actually my 4-wood. So, the shot put me closer to the hole and I could 2-putt, I used my head. For a Puerto Rican, that's pretty good thinking."
Chi Chi Rodriguez

"You can make a balata ball stop more quickly but only if you have the ability. It's like owning a pair of spiked running shoes when all you have the ability to do is jog."

David Graham

HISTORY and TRADITIONS

"That Fute ball and Golfe be utterly cryit doune, and nocht usit."

An attempt by King James II of Scotland to ban golf in 1457

"No catall scal haf pastour of gyrss apone the lynkis."

The first reference to "links" in the Aberdeen Register in 1487

"Playing of the gowff on the links of Leith every Sabbath the time of the sermonses."

The crime for which John Henrie and Pat Rogie were imprisoned in Edinburgh in 1593

1. You must tee your ball within one club's length of the hole.
2. Your tee must be on the ground.

The first two Rules of the Gentlemen Golfers, 1744

"Come out and finish the match or I'll play the remaining holes and claim the stakes."

Willie Park to his great rival Old Tom Morris, who chose to end their great rivalry by staying in a pub having a drink rather than finish the match

"If you believe in reincarnation I was probably a Scotsman 250 years ago."

Lee Trevino

"All that man can do is to beat those who are around when he is around. He cannot beat those who went before or those who are yet to come."

Bobby Jones on posterity

"One of sport's oldest stories concerns the golfer who threw his clubs into the sea after a painfully bad round and almost drowned trying to rescue them."

Herbert Warren Wind, golf writer

"People have been playing golf for 300 years longer than they've been playing the piano."

Charles Price

"Their zenith was the zenith of the exhibition match. They were constantly playing against one another and no matter on what mud-heap they met, the world really cared which of them won."

Bernard Darwin on the "Great Triumvirate" Taylor, Vardon and Braid

"Vardon was the most atrocious putter I have ever seen. He didn't 3-putt he 4-putted."

Gene Sarazen on Vardon in the early 1920s when he suffered from the "yips"

"Until Hagen and Gene Sarazen came along American golf existed in a vacuum. American golfers stood with their backs to the Atlantic and either didn't know or didn't care that the game had any roots."

Fred Corcoran

"If in 1931 you had been, say, 19 – as Snead, Nelson and Hogan then were – you would be hard put to think of a profession with less promise than that as a golfer. Lion tamer would have made sense, and riding a barrel over Niagara Falls might have got your mother's blessing. But not golf."

Charles Price

"Golf was not particularly well served by its early historians. Most of them were journalists and Scots, nothing wrong with either. But the combination of the two conditions meant they had a compulsion to distort or ignore facts which conflicted with their paramount article of faith, namely that golf was invented by Scots, in Scotland, without any help or interference from outlanders."

Peter Dobereiner

"When you first have a chance to win a Major, it is like facing a wall you have to destroy. And when you have done it once, you can destroy any other wall you face in future."

Jose Maria Olazabal

"Most of us would give up our wives, our firstborn and our favourite putters just to finish in the top ten in a Major."
Lee Trevino

"How many Majors did you win?"
Gene Sarazen's idea of the only relevant question to test the brilliance of a professional golfer

"To learn to win major championships you have to learn to lose major championships."
Tom Watson

"No matter how much the Tournament Players Championship covets similar status, tradition cannot be painted onto a championship as a coat of paint is added to a wall."
John Hopkins on the latter day pretensions of the TPC to be "The Fifth Major"

"In a regular tournament you can say 'I'm going to give this 100%', but there's not that same feeling inside. Your concentration is not spot-on all the time. In a Major, the sum total of your physical and mental attitude seems to be greater."
Nick Faldo

"Majors are not the only measure of golfing success . . . Who made the Majors major anyhow."
Ian Woosnam before winning the Masters

IMAGE

"Men should always play in their braces."
Harry Vardon

"He knew that making money from golf did not depend only on winning titles. It depended on being noticed, talked about, quoted, criticised – anything, in fact, but ignored."
Henry Longhurst on Walter Hagen

"Hagen was the original clothesman of the links, a man who realised that the way a player dressed could act as a strong pyschological weapon in his favour . . . Hagen showed the world that golf needn't be an excuse for appearing in the gardener's cast-offs."

Writer Geoffrey Dickinson

"I've noticed some of them are off balance when they swing. They're top heavy. They've got too much hair."

Ben Hogan on pro golfers in 1970

"I feel calm in calm colours. I don't want people to watch me the way I dress. I want people to watch me the way I play."

Severiano Ballesteros on his dress code

"Man, I've got to blow-dry my hair or I've got to withdraw from the tournament. I don't play anywhere unless I can blow-dry my hair."

A very young Ben Crenshaw

"In 1962, the year I came onto the tour, just out of Ohio State, I'm telling you that you'd have found a better dressed guy out of a refugee camp than what I was; I was some sort of bad dresser. In the Open I was wearing a pair of twelve-dollar retail pants, iridescent olive-green-blue like the belly colour of a bottle-fly."

Jack Nicklaus

"I'm not colour blind like Jack, I can pick out my own colours."

Johnny Miller (Nicklaus is actually colour blind)

"Women are women, and I doubt if any of them really take up golf in that holy, quest-of-the-grail spirit which animates men. I have known girls to become golfers as an excuse for wearing pink jumpers, and one, at least, who did it because she had read in the beauty hints in the evening paper that it made you lissom. Girls will be girls."

PG Wodehouse

"I wanted people to recognise me for my character and my quality of play not for the guy with diamonds in his teeth."

Calvin Peete on why he had his trademark diamonds removed

"If you don't send me a couple of hundred pounds a week, I'm going to start wearing your clothes."
Threat issued by pro Simon Hobday, nicknamed "Scruffy", to a clothing manufacturer

"You bastard. I came out here with all new, clean clothes and I didn't think you would recognise me with a crease in my trousers."
Simon Hobday howling at some malevolent Deity after 3-putting the first green in a Seniors event in California

"I'd give up golf if I didn't have so many sweaters."
Bob Hope

"Today's golfer believes that by buying clubs with Arnold Palmer's name stamped on them he is purchasing some degree of his skill. The assumptions in this subconscious train of thought are too foolish to enumerate, but the effect is a powerful marketing force. In the same way, but even more absurdly, Bill Casper shirts, Lee Trevino hats, and Gary Player slacks are jujus to us sophisticated golfers."
Peter Doberiener

"He's tremendously confident right now. He'd need to be to dress the way he does."
Colin Montgomerie on Payne Stewart

"(He) gets some of his ideas by going behind the counter of a chemist's shop, looking through the brightly-coloured pills and tablets in the bottles and then sending any particular colour combination of pills to his tailor for matching and making up."
Geoffrey Dickinson on Doug Sanders

"It looks like he needs to stand a little closer to his razor in the mornings."
Mark McCormack on John Daly

A PRO'S LOT

"A bunch of vagabonds who (wear) polyester pants for a living."
Peter Jacobsen's description of professional golfers

"Pain and suffering are inevitable in our lives, but misery is an option."
  Chip Beck

"The life of a professional athlete is precarious at best. Win and they carry you to the clubhouse on their shoulders; lose and you pay the caddies in the dark."
  Gene Sarazen

"Golf Pro: An optimistic doctor who has a cure for dying."
  Jim Bishop

"There are two types of golf – golf and tournament golf. The latter is an ageing game."
  Bobby Jones

"Casual golf and tournament golf are as different as ice hockey and tennis."
  Ben Hogan

"I've seen players hang around these ropes for years, ducking under and coming in and asking me, tournament after tournament, and they never make the cut. Think of that. And people play this game for fun. Oh my!"
  One-time US PGA official scorekeeper Dom Mirandi

"I'm a hot dog pro. That's when someone in the gallery looks at his pairing sheet and says, 'Here comes Joe Baloney, Sam Sausage and Chi Chi Rodriguez. Let's go get a hot dog.'"
  Chi Chi Rodriguez

"Even if you play bad golf . . . I mean, you could be hanging to a subway strap."
  Rocky Thompson

"You start thinking about winning on Saturday night and you're going to shoot 80 on Sunday."
  Olin Browne, US Nike Tour player

"When I sashay down the final fairway I always have tears in my eyes. I feel like a pilgrim entering Plymouth harbour."
  Mac O'Grady waxing lyrical

"Amateur golf don't mean shit."
Mike Hill, US veteran, to Peter Teravainen on the record of a talented amateur turned pro

"Spurs getting relegated."
Professional golfer Russell Claydon on his worst fear

"Golf, especially championship golf, isn't supposed to be any fun, was never meant to be fair, and never will make any sense."
Charles Price

"I once killed a water moccasin snake in a pro-am. I played that hole really badly all week, so now I leave all animals alone. If a fly lands on my ball, I stand waiting until it flies away."
Hubert Green on his peculiar superstition

"I have to wear a white shirt with a stripe, any kind of stripe, as long as it's not red, but I'm not superstitious."
Chi Chi Rodriguez

"I had to take the rabbit's foot out eventually, because it smelt too much."
Mark Roe on his former talisman

"Imagine if you had to play below your handicap on six consecutive days to retain your club membership."
David Jones on the European Tour Qualifying School

"It was the most terrifying week I've ever spent. The only part of my body that stayed loose was my bowels . . . if you blow the Tour qualifier, you start practising lines for your next job, such as, 'Would you like paper or plastic, sir?' or 'Those wiper blades look a little worn.'"
Peter Jacobsen on the US PGA Tour qualifying tournament

"The tournament lasted a year. It was a nightmare. People were bleeding to death. Ultimately my experience saw me through."
David Feherty on the Qualifying School

"I never knew what top golf was like until I turned professional – then it was too late."
Steve Melnyk

"Them that don't win, they're haberdashers. They sell sweaters and slacks and call themselves pros."

George Low

"Golfers who know, buy from their Pro."

Slogan of the Professional Golfers Co-Operative Association

"Playing on the American tour is like being in the Army. You always have to ask the Captain for permission to visit somewhere else in the world."

Seve Ballesteros

"Hi George, welcome to Europe."

Greg Norman to a PGA European tour official (George Grady) at the Johnny Walker Classic in Singapore

"There's an old saying on Tour, 'Set fire to the trees and cover the greens with broken glass, put the pros out there in gasoline-soaked pants and barefoot, and someone will break par.'"

Tommy Bolt

"These are the finest flagsticks I have ever seen anywhere in the world."

Gary Player, apparently being quite serious, about the Dalmahoy flagsticks

"Discuss the stock market. Talk about your families. Tell jokes. Have a soda."

David Graham's remedy for dealing with slow play ahead

"The bang was so loud when we hit the overhang that our Persian cat, Cleo, jumped about two feet in the air and screeched in my face. When we backed out, the whole awning tore off . . . and they talk about the glamour of the tour."

Paul Azinger after his wife wedged their motor home in a toll booth during his early days on the tour

"When I roomed with him in South Africa, Simon designated Monday as washday. That meant filling a bath with water, pouring in a liberal amount of detergent, emptying in the entire contents of his suitcase and then proceeding to stir the lot with a putter. When he felt the clothes had been stirred sufficently, they were thrown out on the balcony to dry."

Roddy Carr talking to Dermot Gilleece of the Irish Times *on the laundering arrangements of Simon Hobday, nicknamed "Scruffy"*

"When I'm hitting the ball well, I don't see how I could ever have hit it poorly. But when I'm in a slump, I don't know how I ever could have hit the ball well."

Tom Weiskopf on elusive form

"Why do I love kids so much? Because I was never a kid myself. I was too poor to be a child, so I never really had a childhood. The biggest present I ever got was a marble."

Chi Chi Rodriguez

"I used to dream that I could be a waiter in a place like this."

Chi Chi Rodriguez on Butler National GC in Illinois

"The players themselves can be classified roughly into two groups – the attractions and the entry fees."

Jimmy Demaret

"Guys from Texas and Florida usually are good wind players. Californians? We're usually good at buying Mercedeses and ordering dinner at expensive restaurants."

Broadcaster and pro Gary McCord

"I didn't realise at the moment exactly what I had done . . . I only realised the enormity of it when I walked into the press room and got a long, standing ovation. It wasn't until I came out of my daze that I began to appreciate my accomplishment."

Al Geiberger after shooting a 59 in the 1977 Memphis Open talking about what players call, the "Zone"

"Sometimes guys have personality transplants after they win a Major, or they assume their IQ rises as they climb up the money list."

Peter Jacobsen

"I've never had one."

Ronan Rafferty on being asked in an interview what was his first job

"This is my office. I love my office."
Chi Chi Rodriguez's description of the golf course

"Seventy-five per cent of players on the European Tour are clones who do not know on which side their bread is buttered."
Brian Barnes

"Bet you've never heard of a tour player striking because they wouldn't give him the weekends off?"
Tommy Bolt

"Statisticians estimate that the average rate of crime among good golfers is lower than in any class of the community except possibly bishops. Since Willie Park won the first championship at Prestwick in the year 1860 there has, I believe, been no instance of an Open Champion spending a day in prison."
PG Wodehouse's "The Oldest Member"

"There are seemingly only three professions where you do not lose your job for consistent poor performance: TV weathermen in the UK, tournament professional golfers and the PGA officials who set flag positions."
Tony Johnstone of Zimbabwe

"I have always said that because European golfers learn to play with so many clothes on – you know, long-sleeved shirts, three sweaters, insulated underwear and rain gear – that Hell, they did not know how good they were until they came over here and started pulling all that stuff off."
Trevino on European players

"My Turn-Ons: big galleries, small scores, long drives, short rough, fat pay cheques and skinny trees."
Peter Jacobsen

Fifteenth Hole: Fourth Estate Par 3

Hole: 15th Portmarnock
Par 3 187 yds
Designer: WC Pickeman/Mungo Park & others

The pallid, rotund man eased himself out of his wooden chair and padded across the carpet-tiled floor to the coffee dispenser. Pouring himself a cup he eyed the wilting cucumber sandwiches with distaste.

"Any ham?" He asked the girl behind the counter. "You said there'd be ham by three o'clock. Where is it?"

"It's on the way, sir, sorry."

He snapped his head in irritation and floundered back towards the long table with the green baize cloth. Slurping a mouthful of coffee he athletically dialled a number on his phone. 0044 . . . As he did so he squinted at the large board which dominated the marquee. The canvas of the tent fluttered in the light breeze behind him.

"Faldo – 5 under after 9." He always adopted his most guttural tone when he spoke to base.

"6 under after 11," came the bored reply from the other end. "Why don't you watch it on TV, like the rest of us?"

"Look, old chap, I'm OUT there. Getting colour, texture, the whites of their eyes . . . you can't get all that and be bang up to date, right?"

"Right! When were you out on the course last? Strutting your stuff during the pro-am?"

"Piss off." He hung up abruptly. He lit a Marlboro. Always had to be a Marlboro.

An energetic young radio reporter swept past, radiating awareness.

"Moron!" muttered the Hack. "Local radio, obituaries for obese housewives."

Startled by his own imagery, he glanced down at his paunch and promised himself to start doing something about it. "Monday . . . yes,

Monday. Soon as this one's over."

The battery-operated radio reporter tapped him on the shoulder.

"Have you not heard? Lightning at the 12th, suspected heart attack!"

"Tell them to bring the body into the press tent, old chap," he said, summoning as much condescension as he was capable of, "and then it'll be news."

A quick shrug of the shoulders and Marconi was gone, leaving behind the lingering stench of enthusiasm. Outside there was a hubbub. The Hack glanced up. Seve! Back in form, a 64. About bloody time he'd arrived. That little shit from Irish TV had obviously got to him first. See about that! Self-important ponce!

The PGA press man ushered the tall tanned Spaniard to the table at the end of the interview room. The Hack elbowed his way past the home contingent and took up his pew in the front row.

"Could you take us through your card, please, Seve?" This from the PGA buff.

"First hole – Drive – 7-iron – 2 putts . . . "

Eighteen holes later and . . . with one or two embellishments . . . it would run nicely. Time for the quote! As the Spaniard wound down the pencil was hoisted. Time to paste on the charm. The Hack allowed himself the merest hint of a congratulatory smile as he asked . . . "Seve, your best round this year . . . how do you feel?"

ON THE BOX

"I don't mind that booth. That's pretty good money. I almost finish third every week I'm up there."
Lee Trevino

"To illustrate how difficult this shot is, go out into your front yard and chip a ball from your lawn down onto the hood of your car and make it stop. Pretty hard to do, huh? Well this is tougher."
Broadcaster Gary McCord on the 16th at Muirfield Village

"It's funny. You need a fantastic memory in this game to remember the great shots, and a very short memory to forget the bad ones."
Gary McCord

"(It's) almost as if the commentators were being paid by the word. I confess that when I hear of their salaries I sometimes think they are."
Peter Alliss on American commentators

"The son-of-a-bitch went in!"

Jimmy Demaret's radio comment after Lew Worsham sank a 120-yard wedge shot to win the 1953 World Championship of Golf by one stroke

"The sand and dirt did wonders for my voice. My periodic updates sounded like Joe Cocker with a head cold."

Peter Jacobsen on covering the 1991 Ryder Cup Match at Kiawah Island

"I got the feeling many years ago that Frank firmly believes that he and he alone is the only person in the entire universe who knows how golf should be covered. Anyone who disagrees with him is either a complete idiot or a charlatan."

Peter Alliss on CBS Golf producer Frank Chirkinian

"One thing different about us compared to the BBC is that we don't sit on our arses watching the grass grow."

Frank Chirkinian

"Television will get round to showing the highlights in a few months – on the second national channel."

Seve Ballesteros, after one of his Masters wins, commenting wryly on the lack of enthusiasm for golf in Spain

McKay: "Well, by the look of Craig, it's pretty warm out there."
Marr: "It certainly is, and from the looks of that shirt, he's been dressed by the dreaded sisters, Polly and Ester."

Jim McKay and Dave Marr watching a profusely perspiring Craig Stadler on ABC

"I like to have sex, what do you do?"

Wayne Riley after being asked by the BBC radio golf correspondent Tony Adamson what he liked doing when he wasn't playing golf

"I'm really going to do my homework . . . I'm going to be down there on the practice tee before the telecast, finding out if a guy's wife beat him up the night before. Important stuff like that. Stuff that people want to know."

Lee Trevino on becoming a TV commentator

"Lie? I've got no fucking lie. I don't even have a fucking shot."
Miller Barber's response to a civil question from Ken Venturi on CBS

"RTE is not like one of the hustle-bustle American networks: it is laid back almost to the horizontal."
Peter Dobereiner on the national channel's golf coverage

Radio Reporter: "Excuse me, David, have you got a word for me?"
Feherty: "Yes, balls! Will that do?"
An exchange involving the inimitable Mr F

"Once initiated into the black art the tyro radio reporter can cope with every contingency without having to seek recourse in any process of thought. Come the arrest of a serial killer, the birth of sextuplets or the winning of the Open Championship, all he has to do is pronounce the sacred radio mantra: 'How does it FEEL?'"
Peter Dobereiner

"He's been in more spots than Bob Hope."
Gary McCord on the much-travelled American pro Tom Lehman

"Peter is overly critical, harsh with some of his comments. In my view he tries to put himself above the players."
Jacklin on Peter Alliss

"Unless you happen to be Peter Alliss, silence is likely to be more eloquent than anything you can think of to say."
Peter Dobereiner's advice to golf broadcasters

"And now from London, England, that well-known professional, Olive Clark."
American announcer getting Clive Clark's name wrong in a pro-am

"They're ripping it at the flag, of course I guess that's where the hole is."
Ken Venturi on CBS

"Hey, aren't you the guy that does the 16th at the Masters?"
American airline passenger to Henry Longhurst

"I bowed to his authority on golfing topics and he graciously deferred to me in the matter of settling the bill on our frequent visits to the bar, an arrangement from which I was the major beneficiary."
    Peter Dobereiner on Henry Longhurst

"He . . . had a very leery attitude to making mistakes, mispronouncing names, and committing spoonerisms. The prospect of Hunt and Coles being drawn together, playing together and having to be mentioned in his commentary always struck a good deal of fear into him."
    Peter Alliss on friend and colleague Henry Longhurst

"Tell Longhurst there is no 'p' in Thomson."
    Caller to the BBC during an Open play-off between Peter Thomson and Dave Thomas

"I just don't know about the guy. He looks like WC Fields in drag. But he happens to be the best in the business."
    Frank Chirkinian on Henry Longhurst

"Like a fall of Yorkshire soot."
    Unattributed comment on the vocal qualities of John Jacobs's golf commentary

"Winged Foot has the toughest 18 finishing holes in golf."
    Dave Marr on ESPN

THE PRESS

"The journalist in me said I should go back and get his name. The golfer in me said 'Fuck him'."
    Joe Gordon of the Boston Herald *after eagling the 15th at Augusta, standing on the 16th to be told that a member of the group behind had just had an albatross*

"Wouldn't you think the guy who 'knows every blade of grass on the course' would know how far it was to the hole?"
    George Kimball on Nicklaus upbraiding his young caddy at the 3rd hole on Mount Juliet's opening day because he got the yardage wrong

"If someone dropped an atom bomb on the 6th hole, the press would wait for a golfer to come in and tell them about it."
Ben Hogan

"Thus the sentence, 'This is a magnificent test of golf' can be translated as, 'I hold the course record'. Likewise when Dave Hill is quoted as saying, 'This course is nothing but a cow pasture' he is really saying, 'I missed the cut'. Beware too of Gary Player's favourite quote: 'This is the finest golf course I have ever seen, of its kind.' That is verbal shorthand for 'The commissioner has warned me that the next time I criticise a host club in public he will have my guts for garters.'"
Peter Dobereiner on the subtext at players press conferences

"No one is interested in what Faulkner thinks about the way he played. They want to know how I think he played."
The great journalist Bernard Darwin at the 1951 British Open where one of the earliest winner's press conferences took place

"I hate abroad."
Bernard Darwin

"Where's Tom McCollister? Thanks Tom!"
Nicklaus after winning the 1986 Masters. McCollister had written that Nicklaus was "washed up" and helped inspire the Golden Bear to victory.

"I'm going to write a piece next week about how I won the Masters for Jack Nicklaus."
Tom McCollister, Atlanta Constitution

"I used to work on the letters page, and play round Royal Wimbledon some mornings before going to work. The editor was walking along the corridor enquiring of the sports editor who was going to replace Bernard Darwin as golf correspondent. The sports editor looked up, saw me, and said, 'He plays golf, let's give him a go'."
The Times *correspondent Peter Ryde on the rigorous selection process which earned him the job*

"It is necessary to invent quotes more and more these days because professional golfers are gradually losing the power of speech. Already adverbs have been eliminated entirely from their vocabulary. 'I hit the ball super but putted just horrible.'"

Peter Dobereiner

Reporter: "Lee, what are your immediate plans?"
Trevino: "To run one of you guys over if you don't get the hell out of my way."

Trevino being questioned in the Augusta car park

"OK Charlie, let's start this again, shall we?"

Nick Faldo interrupted in mid stroke by the accidental clicking of photographer Charles Briscoe-Knight's camera

"Arnie, do you consider it would be going too far to describe yourself as a has-been?"

Reporter to Palmer in the press tent during the Masters

"Sic transit Gloria Monday."

Henry Longhurst's reference to the first round defeat of Gloria Minoprio in the English Women's Championship

"Sic transit Gloria Tuesday."

His tag on the only occasion on which she made it into the second round, where she lost

"They do an excellent job, considering the fact that they're writing about something about which they know nothing."

US pro Frank Beard on the gentlemen and women of the Fourth Estate

"On a wet Thursday afternoon when the golf is less than riveting and boredom, even disenchantment, with the job threatens, there is always a voice of sanity somewhere in the press tent eager to point out the afternoon shift at Frickley Colliery has just started work."

Bill Elliot

"Not to have read Dan Jenkins on golf is like playing golf in Scotland and missing out Carnoustie."

John Hopkins

Reporter: "Do you think the guys can shoot low on this course, Arnie?"
Palmer: "Well, any time you drive the ball in the fairway, hit all the greens and make a bunch of putts, then you have a chance to make a score."

Arnold Palmer being blindingly obvious in response to a blindingly obvious press question

"The last time I birdied the first hole, I tried to lay up for the next 17."

Journalist Charles Price showing that not many writers can play the game either

"You mustn't talk when we play."

A very young Seve scolding (unwittingly) Guardian *golf correspondent Pat Ward Thomas*

"The professional golf-watcher never catches the action. I could write a volume on Great Moments in Golf I Have Missed."

Peter Dobereiner

"You guys write crap!"

Ian Woosnam in the press tent during the 1991 Open

"You begin to wonder, when the same guy who stitched you up last week wants to talk to you the next."

Ronan Rafferty, whose relations with the press have often been chequered

"Golf is growing without me and whether or not Ronan Rafferty talks to the press is not going to effect that expansion."

Ronan Rafferty

"Getting an interview with Ronan Rafferty is . . . a bit like hunting a killer whale. You have to be prepared to go in search of it day after day without reward."

Jock Howard, Golf World

"I've come to the conclusion that however good you try to be, and however hard you work, someone's still going to have a knife in for you. Ignorance is a dangerous thing when you've got a pen in your hand and a lot of readers."

Tony Jacklin on the press

"I'd like to thank the press from the bottom of my . . . well from the heart of my bottom anyway."

Faldo stooping to the level of some of his press antagonists in his speech after winning the 1992 Open at Muirfield

"The press all want you to be a nice guy and go to the bar and have a beer, but if you say anything while you are there they will kill you. And if you think, 'Well I won't go to the bar', they kill you for that. Then you are a miserable bastard who won't even go to the bar. You can't win."

Faldo on the frustration of dealing with golf writers and broadcasters

"No Comment."

Howard Clark in response to a cheerful "Good Morning" from a golf journalist

"I mean, all of a sudden you are supposed to know everything. They ask you who is going to be the next President, who's going to win the baseball, what's wrong with this golfer – it's almost embarrassing because it's not worth answering. They think if you are the No 1 golfer, you are the No 1 know-it-all."

Fred Couples on the debit side of his 1992 Masters win

LITERATURE

"O! pardon me, thou bleeding piece of earth." (*Julius Caesar*)
"Put in their hands the bruising irons of wrath." (*Richard III*)
"Give me the iron, I say." (*King John*)
"Three misbegotten knaves in Kendal Green came at my back and let drive at me." (*Henry IV Part One*)
"To mourn a mischief that is past and gone
Is the next way to draw new mischief on." (*Othello*)

Clear and unambiguous references to golf in the works of Shakespeare

"It's good sportsmanship to not pick up lost golf balls while they are still rolling."

Mark Twain

"I'm not sure if dancing is a good thing for a fellow's game. You never hear of any first class pro dancing. James Braid doesn't dance."

PG Wodehouse in "A Mixed Threesome"

"The first one is called 'How to Get the Most Distance out of your Shanks' and the other is 'How to Take the Correct Stance on your Fourth Putt'."

Lee Trevino on his two latest golf books

"When hitting wedge shots, I've a flair
That's turning my hair grey;
They stop, I swear, right next to where,
The pin was . . . yesterday."

Dick Emmons

"Oh some in coats o' cruel red,
An' some in tartan knicks
An' some wid ties o' chaney blue,
Bud all o' thim wid sticks.
An' they batter at a weenie ball
That's lyin' on the sod
An' hits it – no! they hammers it,
An' digs out pounds of clod.
If the ball wint wid the surface thin
Them two'd complate the scene
But no! Its sleepin' where it lay,
Like a mushroom, white and clean.
It's the most uprooted coun-thery
That iver yit was seen:
From Aughnacloy to Kinnegar
They're slicin' off the green."

Verse of an epic poem by Dr WF Collier of the Royal Belfast Club, written in the 1890s

"A steady putt and then it went
Oh, most securely in.
The very turf rejoiced to see
That quite unprecedented three."

Sir John Betjeman

"It was a morning when all nature shouted 'Fore!' The breeze, as it blew gently up from the valley, seemed to bring a message of hope and cheer, whispering of chip shots holed and brassies landing squarely on the meat. The fairway, as yet unscarred by the irons of a hundred dubs, smiled greenly up at the azure sky; and the sun, peeping above the trees, looked like a giant golf-ball perfectly lofted by the mashie of some unseen god and about to drop dead by the pin of the eighteenth."

PG Wodehouse

Sixteenth Hole: Real Estate Par 4

Hole: 16th K Club
Par 4 394 yds
Designer: Arnold Palmer & Ed Seay

You've never cheated at golf before so the perturbation of your spirit threatens to spoil your enjoyment of the round on which you are about to embark, on a course you have longed to play over ever since you saw the first computer enhanced layout. Your lust, your desire, to penetrate the dark mysteries of the Smorgasbord Course at Ordeal Canyon has driven you to steal your best friend's handicap certificate. You are a steady 6 handicapper, nowhere near expert enough to be allowed within the electrified perimeter fence of the course which has been described by John Daly as being "as long as an Oklahoma winter". Only plus handicappers need bother approach the Course Supervisor (Obergruppenfuhrer von Kleist, a former Gauleiter from the Waffen SS). Why? Because this is the ultimate, 18 holes designed by 18 of the world's most revered golf course architects. It's as if the entire Impressionist school had combined on a Paint-By-Numbers Old Master. As if Joyce, Proust and Jeffrey Archer had collaborated on a whodunnit.

You tee off on the 1st, shaking like a Japanese multi-storey car park in a 7.5 trembler. It's a Pete Dye par 3, with a 250-yard carry over a lake to a kidney-shaped green protected from erosion by vertical railway sleepers. The tee on which you stand is entirely composed of horizonatal railway sleepers. The green at which you take aim with your driver consists entirely of diagonal railway sleepers. You've been told they have a stimpmeter reading of 26, twice as fast as Augusta.

You give up after your fifth ball lands on the green and falls back into the water and move onto the 2nd hole. This is a Robert Trent Jones Sr par 4, a real monster at 499 yards. Your drive requires a blind shot across a mound inspired by the tumulus at Newgrange in

County Meath. Having safely negotiated that, you face a second shot from a sharp downhill lie, across three pot bunkers and another mound to a plateau green which you can see on your Strokesaver but have no other visible evidence actually exists. Judging the distance remaining to the green to be about 250 yards you decide to risk a 3-wood, despite the lie. You catch it beautifully and immediately regret you didn't take a driver.

Your ball is now lying about 70 yards from the front of the elevated green, which falls 12 feet from front to back. Better to be short, you think, putting yourself in the mind of Mr Trent Jones, whom you know likes intelligent golfers who play intelligent golf. Your pitch is perfect, landing 2 feet from the pin . . . before it stops and begins to roll back down the slope towards you. You try again, this time you pitch past the flag and the ball is back at your feet more quickly.

Ten shots later you calmly replace your wedge in the bag, put the ball in your pocket, tear up your best friend's handicap certificate and walk off the course, opting to miss out on the Tom Fazio snake-infested 3rd which involves a triple cross over three canyons, the Jack Nicklaus-designed 4th where your drive must clear a Giant Redwood pine forest before coming to rest just short of a Grade-Three river . . . and so on. As you leave you see an ashen-faced Tom Watson telling a reporter it was about as easy as getting pregnant. You feel somewhat consoled.

DESIGNERS

"A perfect tee shot should make the following shot less difficult; a perfect second shot should only be probable after the perfect first. Each step of the journey should be hazardous; the links should be almost too difficult for the players."

John Low in "Concerning Golf", 1903

"Every natural obstacle (is) to be used and there should be complete variety of holes in length and character and design. Putting greens should always be well guarded and the shorter the hole, the smaller the green should be."

James Braid, "Advanced Golf", 1908

"I am sick to death of seeing so many thirty-by-thirties in greens and ten-by-tens in tees."
The great designer HS Colt arguing against uniformity

"A great course should have the Atlantic Ocean on one side, the Pacific on the other, and Ben Hogan or Arnold Palmer winning a tournament on it."
Pete Dye sounding like he's suggesting only great golf courses can be built in Panama

"There are as many course architects as there are golfers. Everyone is an architect in his Walter Mitty dreams."
Robert Trent Jones Jr

"Man, I don't want any of this golf course design business. When I wake up in the morning all I want to do is slap that rubber ball."
Lee Trevino

"The first hole should never count."
The reported reasoning behind the construction by Chi Chi Rodriguez of a 19-hole course in Puerto Rico

"I want to build courses people enjoy playing so you can take your wife and family out and have a good time. I don't build monuments to myself."
Arnold Palmer in response to a question about Nicklaus-designed courses

"I don't know. I frankly have never seen one of his golf courses. He doesn't do a lot of courses. His people do a lot of courses."
Nicklaus responding to a question about Palmer-designed courses

"McDonald laid out the course so that the holes marched clockwise around the perimeter of the golf club's plot. The golfer who hooked on any hole ended up in heavy rough . . . Old Charley, of course, never hooked. He had a fine grooved slicy swing, and when he sliced there was always ample room out there on the right to take good care of his ball. The old boy was unbeatable on his own course for years."
Herbert Warren Wind on Charles Blair McDonald, designer of America's first 18-hole course, the Chicago Golf Club, in Wheaton, Illinois

"Golf has . . . afforded me an opportunity permitted few men: to create on one of the broadest canvasses known to man and, in doing so, to complement and, sometimes, to improve on the work of the greatest Creator of all. Golf courses are built by men, but God provides the venues."

The modest claims of Robert Trent Jones Sr

"The man who hates golfers is what they call me. They couldn't be more wrong. I design holes that are fun to play."

Robert Trent Jones Sr

"Early golf courses had no bunkers. They are a strictly man-made invention and the larger ones, such as those that stretch across an entire dairy farm, were the invention of a demented man named Robert Trent Jones."

Dan Jenkins

"No lost balls!"

Point 10 of Dr Alistair McKenzie's 13-point plan for the ideal golf course

"You have to play a course before you can really judge its quality. After all, you don't know whether you like a woman until you sleep with her."

Spanish architect Pepe Gancedo

"Great golf courses should have at least one silly hole."

Frank Hanigan, USGA official

"Building a golf course is my total expression. My golf game can only go on so long. But what I have learned can be put into a piece of ground to last beyond me."

Jack Nicklaus

"A great golf hole is one which puts a question mark into the player's mind when he arives on the tee to play it."

McKenzie Ross, British designer

"I thought I had encountered every hazard but on this course you have to take into account the curvature of the earth."

David Feherty on Crooked Stick during the 1991 US PGA

"You had better learn to count."
Pete Dye on the prospect of playing off the back tees at his Kiawah Island monster

"Dye's true hallmark is the use of railroad ties, telephone poles or planking to shore up greens, sand traps and the banks of water hazards. He uses so much wood that one of his courses may be the first ever to burn down."
Journalist Barry McDermott on Pete Dye

"A good golf course is like good music. It is not necessarily a course which appeals the first time one plays it."
Alister McKenzie

"There are no straight lines on my courses. The good Lord never drew a straight line."
Jack Nicklaus

"Jack, you've built a house without any windows."
Ed Sneed to Jack Nicklaus on Muirfield Village

"Nicklaus is becoming such a prolific golf architect that he's got new projects going everywhere. I finally found a spot where he hadn't built one – in a leper colony."
Bob Hope

DESIGNEES

"A decade from now, I think target golf will be looked back on as the disco music of golf course architecture. We'll simply laugh and wonder how we could ever have been so light-headed."
Peter Jacobsen

"Well it is outdoors, I'll say that much for it."
Raymond Floyd on a Jack Nicklaus-designed course in Arizona

"You don't often go to a course where they have to unprepare it to host a tournament."
David Feberty on the bulldozing of the outrageous greens at the Robert Trent Jones-designed Golf d'Esterel Club in France, said to have been more extravagantly contoured than Dolly Parton

"These golf architects make me sick. They can't play golf, so they rig the courses so nobody else can play, either."
  Sam Snead

"Now I know I've got Trent Jones in my pocket."
  Lee Trevino after winning two tournaments on Trent Jones-designed courses

"That's how architects make their money, always going back to fix what they don't do right in the first place."
  Lee Trevino

"Every course needs a hole that puckers your rear end."
  Johnny Miller

"If I were designing one for myself, there'd be a dog-leg right on every hole and the first hole wouldn't count. That would be a warm-up hole."
  Lee Trevino

"Very nice course this, but where do the members play?"
  Bobby Jones on the Riviera Golf Club in California

SIGNPOSTING

"GO ARNIE GO"
  Banner being towed behind a plane during a Masters tournament (which Palmer won)

"Hit it here, Ohio Fats."
  Placards carried in the rough by anti-Nicklaus (and pro-Palmer?) golf fans in his early years

"Jack is Back."
  Written on the scoreboard after his 1980 US Open success at Baltusrol

"See this one Nick?"
  Banner at St Andrews in 1988 goading Faldo the day after he refused to play his approach to a fog-obscured 18th in the Dunhill Cup

"NO CAMERAS PLEASE"
Sign often carried by an official following Ben Hogan, who detested them

"No PGA Pros allowed."
Sign posted at Tam O'Shanter Country Club after a row over the All-American Open in 1957

"Warning: Watch for snakes."
Signs on the Tom Fazio-designed Ocean Course at Pelican Hill, California

"Players on foot have no standing on the course."
Sign at Thunderbird Golf Club in California where the buggy is King

"Keep off the grass."
Slightly tongue-in-cheek sign at Australia's Woomera Club where there is virtually none, other than on the greens

"Buena Suarte, compadre."
Note left in Seve's locker by Gary Player on the morning of the final round in the 1980 Masters, Seve's first victory in the event

"Players should pick up bomb and shell splinters from the fairways in order to save damage to the mowers."
Sign on British wartime course

"I just came from America where I go to golf course and learn about a game called, Ah S---"
Poster of Japanese golfer hanging in many pro shops

"Nowadays we have electronically-operated scoreboards and placards carried round with every match – only too often at the 'secure arms' position with the vital information facing the ground."
Henry Longhurst

"Muirfield welcomes careful drivers."
Sign at the course

"Budget Sewer Service Inc – We're No 1 in the No 2 business."
Sign on truck seen at the 1989 US Masters

"One is marked 'Member' of which the R&A has almost as many as the YMCA. Another is marked "Guest", which includes all the members' relatives, all their relatives' friends, and all their friends' relatives."
Charles Price on the multiplicity of badges at the Open championship

"If a ball comes to rest in dangerous proximity to a hippopotamus or crocodile, another ball may be dropped at a safe distance, no nearer the hole, without penalty."
Seen at the Nyanza Club in Africa

"PGA: Praise God Always. Welcome to the US Open."
Message on the lawn of the Evangel Baptist Church, near the Baltusrol Clubhouse

"El secretario y la Junta de este club notifican a los miembros y invitados que ham estado jugando al golf y que desean usar el bar que deleran quirarase los zapatos de golf antes de entrar en este recinto para evitar destrozar la moqueta. Se agradece la cooperacion de los miembros a este respecto."
Notice in Spanish Golf Club. "No spikes" was the English translation carried underneath.

"No Dogs, No Women."
Sign outside clubhouse of well-known south of England club

"Members please check your guns with the receptionist."
Wack Wack Golf Club in Manila

"A stroke may be played again if interrupted by gunfire or sudden explosion."
Local rule in then Rhodesia, c. 1970

PARKLAND vs LINKS

"It left those folding valleys between the sand hills and that unique, crisp, seaside turf designed by Providence for rabbits and golfers."
Henry Longhurst on the sea around the Scottish coast

"Inland golf is often decried, and is certainly not so pleasant as the seaside game, but it is splendid in schooling as a supplement to the more sterling stuff. Most of the fine players of today have played much of their golf on inland greens, and have learned that the shots which are necessary on such links are often expedient on the classic courses."

John Low, golf course designer and theorist

"There is no way of re-educating people, unless they play golf courses such as Ballybunion, or Royal Dornoch or St Andrews and get the flavour of a course that isn't green."

Tom Watson on the sameness of American-style golf courses

"Certainly they are the greenest, which is hardly surprising in a country where housewives habitually peep out of their cottage windows and observe that it is a beautiful day for hanging out the washing to rinse."

Peter Dobereiner on Irish greens

"That is the 'outdoor boarding-school' syndrome – run through a field of nettles in the snow at 5 am, come back to a cold shower and a lump of porridge with salt on it, prefects give you a good flogging, do you good, and sleep with boxing gloves on. Don't believe all that crap – all that does is make you a colonel in the KGB."

The response of Peter Alliss to people who insist that the only REAL golf course is a links course

"We were stationed on the very edge of one of those murderous east coast courses where the greens are small and fast, the wind is a howling menace, and the rough is such that you either play straight or you don't play at all."

George McDonald Frazer, "McAuslan in the Rough"

"When they build a course they just go out and seed a tee, seed a green, mow a fairway between them, and leave the rough the same way it's been for a thousand years and will be for two thousand more."

Ben Hogan on links courses

Seventeenth Hole: Charismatics Par 4

Hole: 17th County Sligo
Par 4 455 yds
Designer: ES Colt

Given time the sterling efforts of the golfing authorities to eliminate all competitors with a spark of originality, flair, danger and adventure will probably succeed. Already copious samples of Nick Faldo's sperm have been extracted from him as he sleeps (hence his occasional unaccountable collapses in the last rounds of tour events) in order that the PGAUSPGAUSGAR&A can clone an entire generation of Faldos who, like winter sunlight, will generate plenty of light, but not an iota of warmth. These "Boys From Brazil" will, in the next millenium, dominate tournament golf. They will shoot identical scores, tie, *en masse*, for first place and necessitate highly complicated and interminable play-offs.

But they won't cause trouble (except in their dealings with the press) and their golfing ability will engage the respect of those few irritating spectators who will still insist on paying in to see "golf in the flesh" rather than watch it on one of the excellent, if rather expensive, new "pay-per-view" channels.

By then John Daly, Seve Ballesteros and Fred Couples (as well as the original and, by then, much mellower Nick Faldo) will be playing on the Senior Tour. They will be running that tour themselves and playing in front of thousands of frenzied septuagenarian spectators who will be encouraging them with shouts of "You're the Man" (by then officially banned on the regular tour) and "Grip it and Rip it, John" (unnecessary on the regular tour where players whose drives travel less than 300 yards are fined for slow play).

They will also be competing for the Biennial Trevino Cup, which pits the Best European Seniors against the best from the USA. The Ryder Cup will, by then, be played behind closed doors at the Campo del Costly Membership in Spain and the Pete Dye Memorial

Railway Track and Country Club in Sheboygan. Because of the similarity in style and imagination of the new generation of golfers, and because satellite TV channels daren't risk offending any potential viewers, no Ryder Cup match will have been won by either side since 1999. The USA, with the biggest audience figures, will have retained the trophy since then.

The Senior Tour will be unique in that it will also cling to the outmoded use of caddies. On the regular Tour golf carts, equipped with lasers which work out the distance to the flag and the borrow on the green (all now made of a derivative of formica and with an obligatory stimpmeter rating of 20+), will have been the norm since a failed attempt by PGA European Tour officials to round up the caddies and give them haircuts.

Strict new rules on the PGA European Tour will insist on all players being blonde and ban any grimacing, smiling or other displays of emotion. Left-handers will have been excluded from competition because of the threat they pose to fixed TV camera positions and the new HQ of the European Tour will be in Clones, County Monaghan.

CADDIES

"No man is a hero to his caddy."
  Dudley Doust

"Real golfers, whatever the provocation, never strike a caddy with the driver . . . The sand wedge is far more effective."
  Unattributed quote

"I don't know why that putt hung on the edge. I'm a clean liver. It must be my caddy."
  US pro Joanne Carner

"Once when I'd been in a lot of bunkers, my caddy told me he was getting blisters from raking so much."
  Joanne Carner

"It's like combat. You want someone you can really depend on."
  Doug Sanders bemoaning the old US tour rule banning professional caddies during the summer months

"In the rules of Golf, a player's caddy is a legal extension of himself, and I think that is precisely how Teravainen saw me. I believe that in his treatment of me, I had the rare opportunity to see exactly how a person treats himself."

Writer Michael Bamberger, who spent six months caddying for Peter Teravainen

"The only time I talk on the golf course is to my caddy, and only then to complain."

Seve Ballesteros

"You put doubt in my mind. If you had told me I'd make it, I'd have made it."

Seve rounding on his then caddy Pete Coleman after going into water off a 1-iron. Coleman had recommended a 3-wood. (Coleman now caddies for Bernhard Langer.)

"Seve is a perfectionist. He needs to take out his frustration and you're the nearest man . . . I didn't mind, I've got thick skin."

The genial Coleman's response to the same incident (Other caddies might not be so charitable)

Vardon: "What on earth shall I take now?"
Caddy: "Well sir, I'd recommend the 4.05 train."

Possibly apocryphal tale of an incident on a bad day for Harry Vardon

Reporter: "How did Lee and Ian play?"
Mitchell: "Right handed, I think."

Trevino's caddy Herman Mitchell after Trevino and Woosnam were paired together in the Masters

"You have to play well when you're partnered with a champion."

Gene Sarazen talking about Skip Daniels, his 1932 Open-winning caddy

"I waved to him as he pedalled happily down the drive, the coat I had given him flapping in the breeze, and there was a good-sized lump in my throat as I thought how the old fellow had never flagged during the arduous grind of the tournament and how he had made good his vow to win a championship for me before he died."

Gene Sarazen on Skip Daniels, his caddy when he won the 1932 Open at Sandwich. They never met again.

American: (Patting down the grass behind his ball) "Is this a brassie lie?"
Caddie: "No! Not yet!"
   Conversation overheard at Royal Dublin

Trevino: (to his ball in flight) "Be up, be up, be up."
Aitchison: "Come down, come down."
Trevino: "Leave it alone Willie! Leave it alone!"
   Trevino and his caddy Willie Aitchison

Judge: (To small boy in court) "Do you know the nature of an oath lad?"
Boy: "Yes, sir, sure I used to be your caddy."
   Quoted in the Irish Golfer *of August 1899*

"I was lying ten and had a 35-foot putt. I whispered over my shoulder, 'How does this one break?' and my caddy said, 'Who cares?'"
   Jack Lemmon during the 1983 Bing Crosby Pro-Am

"Memphis? Are we in Memphis. I thought we were in Fort Worth."
   Caddy Adolphus Hull explaining to Raymond Floyd why he had missed the first five greens in a PGA Tour event

"Don't tell me. Tell my lawyer. That was the best chance I had in a long time of making money."
   Gary Player's caddy Pete Matkovich (in jest) to Player, after he had been disqualified from a tournament for not signing a card for a 67

"In common with royalty, editors and boxing managers, the good caddy instinctively talks of 'we' and 'us' – e.g. 'We was robbed at the 14th' – instead of using the third person. It is indeed a question of the two of us against 'them'."
   Henry Longhurst

"It's not a club ye need, it's a map and a compass."
   Caddy Jimmy Rae to American pro Peter Teravainen on an off-day

"Aye, sir, if you can lift three tons of sand."
   The response of pro Derrick Cooper's caddy on being asked if he would be able to carry a fairway bunker

"Take three damn good shots to get up in two today, sir."
Henry Longhurst's caddy on a very windy day

"Tomorrow you will see a 50-kilo girl carrying a 17-kilo bag for a 100-kilo golfer."
Amused (Occidental) onlooker at a tournament in Japan

"My caddy and I had a difference of opinion about which way the putt broke. He was wrong, but I'm the one who had to take the score."
Hale Irwin

"I started at a dime for fore-caddy work, then a quarter as a caddy. But I got big tips because I had clever toes and my man never had a bad lie."
Chi Chi Rodriguez

"When the wind blows you might as well rip it up. That's where my eyeballs come into it. I can tell you whether it's a 1-club wind or a 2-club wind."
Six-time Open-winning caddy Alfie Fyles on yardage books

"Great shot Mr Palmer, what did you hit?"
Peter Oosterhuis's caddy breaking a cardinal rule in a Ryder Cup game. It cost Bernard Gallacher and Oosterhuis the hole.

"I was putting on this duck act – all calm and controlled on the surface but underneath I was paddling like crazy."
Caddy Phil "Wobbly" Morbey on the first tournament he "won" carrying for DJ Russell

"As a tour caddy, you get to be practically inside the professional golfers head. You are able to get close to the people who are closer to figuring the game out. But the player in you feels a little cheated."
Michael Bamberger

Sarazen: "I'm sorry, Joe, I went to church last Sunday and I prayed and I prayed and I prayed that I should qualify for this championship just one more time."
Caddy: "Well, boss. I don't know how you folks pray when you go to church, but when I pray I keep my head down."
Gene Sarazen after topping a drive to miss qualifying for the 1960 US Open

"I think it's slightly straight, Mr Faulkner."
Advice to Max Faulkner from his caddy

"At 17 my caddy and I were like two dummies. But he's been with me 17 years. Eight years ago he said 'You can't fire me, I know too much about you.'"
Fuzzy Zoeller

"I'm going to win so much money this year my caddy will make the top twenty of the money list."
Lee Trevino in 1973

"The carts. Lee and I have a deal. He walks, I ride."
Trevino's caddy Herman Mitchell on what he likes best about the Senior Tour

"When I ask you what kind of club to use, look the other way and don't answer."
Sam Snead to his caddy before a crucial match

"We work as a team, I hand him the clubs and he makes the shots."
Arnold Palmer's caddy "Ironman" Avery

"My caddy."
Walter Travis, American golfer, when asked about his handicap at the British Amateur in 1904

"If you can't bother usin' what I tell ye, then you can carry the bloody bag yourself."
American Frank Stranahan being dressed down by his caddy in the British Amateur, 1956

"I'm as fresh as a daisy. I've just finished a bottle of brandy and when you win I'll start on a second."
Reply to Max Faulkner who noticed his caddy unsteady on his feet and asked him was he all right

SENIORS

"For never any man was yet so old
But hoped his life one winter more might hold."
17th century English poet John Denham (who was not acquainted with golf)

"This is a mulligan in life."
George Archer on the Senior Tour

"And then the Senior Tour came along and gave us all a second life."
Gary Player

"Old golf pros tend to do one of three things: they go on the Senior Tour or retire to the broadcast booth or become inventors of golf gimmicks guaranteed to shave ten strokes off your game."
Peter Jacobsen

"If I can last out here until I'm 65, I'll be able to retire without ever having held a real job."
US Pro John Brodie

"It's the most fun I've ever had with my clothes on."
Lee Trevino on the Senior Tour

"The Senior Tour is the only place you can get a fresh start but know all the mistakes you made the first time."
Lee Trevino

"No way I'm gonna play with flatbellies when I can play with roundbellies."
Lee Trevino

"We train harder than we did when we were younger – we were silly when we were young. We were going out and having a few pints and staying out late. These old guys are all in bed by nine o'clock, man. They get up at six in the morning, they're stretching, they're going to the spa. You think we did that when we were young? We were just getting home when it was time to tee off."
Lee Trevino

"My God, it looks like a wax museum."
  George Low at his first Seniors event

"I have to figure out a way to take a vacation from a vacation."
  Dave Stockton on the Senior Tour

"Dave Stockton has more confidence than John Elway, Deane Beman and Hillary Clinton combined. Well, forget Hillary. Nobody has that much confidence."
  Rocky Thompson on the man he vied with on the Senior Tour for most birdies

"If ten years ago somebody had told me that a bunch of old farts would be making so much money and playing good golf I would never have believed it."
  Larry Mowry, US Senior

"It's kind of a dead feeling knowing you're playing for second. They ought to have two trophies. One for Jack and one for us."
  Chi Chi Rodriguez on Nicklaus's performances on the US PGA Senior Tour

"When I'll play with him, he'll sometimes hit shots that are way off the charts. He's just not into what he's doing out there. He's thinking about some golf course in Japan or Spain."
  Trevino on Jack Nicklaus's lack of commitment to the Senior Tour

"Am I really beating the best players in the world? No, I'm living in the past. I'm beating a bunch of men who are my age. It's probably better to give up gracefully than to get your head beaten in."
  Jack Nicklaus

"I haven't given it much thought. After all, I won't be eligible for another 42 months, five days and eight and a half hours."
  Butch Baird on being asked whether he'd be joining the Senior Tour

"The courses we play on the American Senior Tour are too easy. When the members come up and say we're playing a shorter course than the one they play daily, that's embarrassing."
  Tom Weiskopf

"You know you're on the Senior Tour when your back goes out more than you do."
Bobby Brue, US Senior pro

"What's nice about our tour is you can't remember your bad shots."
Bobby Brue

"Growing old is mandatory. Growing up is optional."
Tom Wargo, winner of 1993 US PGA Seniors Championship

"I never thought we would have to provide crèche facilities for our members."
Tony Gray, Executive Director of European Senior Tour, on new father Tony Jacklin joining the tour

"Because they don't pay out on Friday or Saturday. Green is the colour of money."
Chi Chi Rodriguez on why he always wears green on the final day of a tour event

"It's the big bear against the little mouse from Puerto Rico."
Chi Chi Rodriguez on facing Nicklaus in a play-off in the 1991 US Seniors Open – he lost

"I can't stand the thought of shooting another 80."
Walter Hagen on why he was retiring

"At my age I don't even buy green bananas."
Arnold Palmer

"I had forgotten just how sweet the click of a ball sounds."
Arnold Palmer after getting a hearing aid at the age of 54

"Anybody who resents Arnold getting more attention than the rest of us doesn't deserve to use his head for more than a hat rack."
Doug Sanders being magnanimous and realistic

"I never thought I'd live to shoot my age. I thought somebody would shoot me first."
Dale Morey

"The older I get the better I used to be."
Lee Trevino

"The older you get the longer you used to be."
Chi Chi Rodriguez

"Some people ask if that's my age and I say 'No, not yet, but I'm getting closer.'"
Fifty-six-year-old Al Geiberger on his nickname, "Mr 59" (He once shot a 59)

"If only I had taken up golf earlier and devoted my whole life to it instead of fooling about with writing stories and things, I might have got my handicap down to under 18."
PG Wodehouse at 92

"If I'm breathing heavy, I'm putting uphill, if I tip over I'm going downhill."
Senior tour pro David Goldman on being asked how he read greens

"Like a lot of the guys on the Senior Tour, I have a furniture problem. My chest has fallen into my drawers."
Billy Casper

"Still play. I play any day the pigeons can land."
Sam Snead at 80 and still playing (In 1992 he shot a 66)

"When you get to my age you can't blame a duff shot on someone talking when you are just about to hit. A whole orchestra could be playing Shostakovich – cannons and all – on the tee beside me and it wouldn't disturb my tempo. These days I can't hear a thing."
Gerald Stanley Pitchforth, aged 91

"Being old has great advantages for a golfer. If you have a bad round your memory is so bad that you have forgotten all about it before you reach the locker room."
Lawrence Batley, aged 82

"Golfing pensioners are quicker than most people think. Mainly because nobody bothers with a practice swing in case it's their last."
Unattributed quote from senior citizen

LEFTIES

"Left handed 1. Having left hand more serviceable than right, using it by preference; awkward, clumsy; ambiguous, double-edged, of doubtful sincerity or validity, ill omened, sinister."
Fowler's Concise Oxford Dictionary

"Being a left-handed golfer is a big advantage. No one knows enough about your swing to mess you up with advice."
Bob Charles

"If God wanted you to putt cross-handed he would have made your left arm longer."
Lee Trevino

"There are those who say there was no perceptible difference between the results of his left-handed mashie and his right-handed ones. He was capable of tearing the flag out of the hole with either."
Charles Price on Vardon

"Never saw one who was worth a damn."
Vardon on lefties

"It'll be nice not to use my fake IDs anymore."
Phil Mickelson on turning 21

JOKERS

"I'm playing like Tarzan and scoring like Jane."
Chi Chi Rodriguez

"Greg's the Great White Shark, but I'm the Loan Shark"
Chi Chi Rodriguez on Greg Norman

"How do I address the ball? I say, 'Hello there ball. Are you going to go in the hole or not?'"
Flip Wilson

"Doesn't he sleep at home?"
David Feherty's comment on being told that Senior Tour player Jerry Barber walks five miles every morning to keep fit

"You should have seen how little I was when I was a kid. I was so small I got my start as a ball marker."
Chi Chi Rodriguez

"If that ball can walk over the water so can I."
Simon Hobday prior to walking into a water hazard after his ball had skipped over it onto the green

"Well it wasn't there when you started."
The speedy Hobday responding to a request from the slower Tony Johnstone to move his shadow

"Don't worry about the first two Jack, that's the best you could have done from that lie."
Gary Player to Nicklaus who had just driven two balls out of bounds and barely kept a third in play

"Well, of course, if it came down to a choice between my wife and the 1-iron . . . I'd miss her."
Gary Player joking with the press after his 1-iron helped him win the 1974 Open

"I play in the low 80s. If it's any hotter than that, I won't play.
American comedian Joe E Louis

"I've seen better swings in a condemned playground."
Arnold Palmer on Bob Hope

Reporter: "What was the turning point, Jimmy?"
Demaret: "When I teed off at ten o'clock!"
Jimmy Demaret after losing ten and eight to Ben Hogan

"I made $7,000 on the tour and spent $100,000. The IRS man sent me a get-well card."
Chi Chi Rodriguez in 1982

"Hey, what's so tough about Hollywood? You get as many mulligans as you need to get it right."
Peter Jacobsen commenting on being asked to do a retake of a shot for the film "Dead Solid Perfect"

"Peter Jacobsen does such great imitations. He must really work on them. Maybe he should spend more time imitating his own swing."

Broadcaster quoted, but not identified, by well-known mimic Jacobsen in his book "Buried Lies"

"I didn't realise how long some of these seniors had been around. Yesterday I saw a guy signing his scorecard with a feather."

Bob Hope

"Give me golf clubs, fresh air and a beautiful partner and you can keep my golf clubs and the fresh air."

Jack Benny

"The last time I left the fairway was to answer the telephone, and it was a wrong number."

Chi Chi Rodriguez

"After all these years it's still embarrassing for me to play on the American Golf Tour. Like the time I asked my caddy for a sand wedge and he came back ten minutes later with a ham on rye."

Chi Chi Rodriguez on his accent

"Give me a banana. I'm playing like a monkey. I might as well eat like one."

Chi Chi Rodriguez

"If you don't shut up, I'm going to tell where you swam across the border."

Doug Sanders to Lee Trevino

Eighteenth Hole: Golf is . . . Par 4

Hole: 18th St Margarets
Par 4 458 yds
Designer: Pat Ruddy & Tom Craddock

" . . . A game which consists in striking a small resilient ball with clubs having heads into a series of holes situated at varying distances on a course with natural or artificial hazards irregularly interposed."
Webster's Dictionary

" . . . a way of testing ourselves while enjoying ourselves."
Arnold Palmer

" . . . like art; it's impossible to be perfect."
Sandra Palmer

" . . . the only sport where a man of 60 can play with the best. That's why golf is such a great game, and no one has ever licked it."
Sam Snead

" . . . a game of expletives not deleted."
Dr Irving A Gladstone

" . . . based on honesty. Where else would someone admit to a 7 on an easy par 3."
Jimmy Demaret

" . . . a game Kings and Presidents play when they get tired of running countries."
Writer Charles Price

" . . . a non-violent game played violently from within."
  Bob Toski

" . . . of games the most mystical, the least earthbound, the one wherein the walls between us and the supernatural are rubbed thinnest."
  John Updike

" . . . like chess . . . a game that is forever challenging but can never be conquered."
  Harvey Penick

" . . . a way of making a man naked."
  Shivas Irons, fictional pro in Michael Murphy's "Golf in the Kingdom"

" . . . a negative sport, telling yourself over and over all the things that can go wrong, then not letting them."
  Tom Watson

" . . . the only game where the worst player gets the best of it. They obtain more out of it with regard to both exercise and enjoyment. The good player gets worried over the slightest mistake, whereas the poor player makes too many mistakes to worry over them."
  David Lloyd George

" . . . an ideal diversion, but a ruinous disease."
  Bertie Charles Forbes, magazine editor

" . . . a game even the masters don't master."
  John Updike

" . . . a humbling game."
  George Low, Scottish professional who played in US at the turn of the century

" . . . a young man's vice and an old man's penance."
  Irvin Cobb, humourist

" . . . a compromise between what your ego wants you to do, what experience tells you to do, and what your nerves let you do."
Bruce Crampton, Australian professional

"A game in which you claim the privileges of age, and retain the playthings of childhood."
Samuel Johnson

" . . . not a game of great shots. It's a game of the most accurate misses. The people who win make the smallest mistakes."
Gene Littler

" . . . a game where the ball always lies poorly and the players well."
Unattributed

" . . . the only sport I know of where a player pays for every mistake. A man can muff a serve in tennis, miss a strike in baseball, or throw an incomplete pass in football, and still have another chance to square himself. But in golf, every swing counts against you."
Lloyd Mangrum

" . . . a way of testing ourselves while enjoying ourselves."
Arnold Palmer

" . . . like driving a car. As you get older you get more careful."
Sam Snead

" . . . 90% inspiration and 10% perspiration."
Johnny Miller

" . . . an awkward set of bodily contortions designed to produce a graceful result."
Tommy Armour

" . . . the Esperanto of sport, the language we all understand."
Henry Longhurst

" . . . a game where guts, stick-to-itiveness and blind devotion will always net you absolutely nothing but an ulcer."

Tommy Bolt

" . . . the great mystery. Like some capricious Goddess it bestows its favours with what would appear to be an almost fat-headed lack of method and discrimination."

PG Wodehouse

" . . . like a razor. You get just so sharp and then it begins to dull a little the more you use it."

Doug Sanders

" . . . the only game in which one can perform on the very battleground on which the mighty have made history, the humble can stand exactly where the great man stood, facing the same problems and their solution may well be superior to the one which, in the event, lost him several thousand pounds."

Henry Longhurst

" . . . the worst damn fun anybody ever had."

Cy Manier, US pro

" . . . a puzzle without an answer."

Gary Player

" . . . only a game, and while I wouldn't want to go out on a theological limb and say that life is also only a game, many of the paradoxes apply."

John Updike

" . . . the most delightful game in the world, so is it also the most difficult. It is easier even for a person who has never handled a gun to learn to become a really good shot than for him who has not lifted a cleek or driver to bloom into a golfer of the first water."

H Rider Haggard

" . . . the loneliest of games, not excluding postal chess."

Peter Dobereiner

" . . . the kind of game you bang yourself over the head with. I've never understood why so many countries want to claim credit for inventing it. I can tell you the Irish have always denied all knowledge of anything like that."

David Feherty

" . . . a good walk spoiled."

Mark Twain

Afterword

Golf – the game we have all given up many times but still come back for more.

The game devised by a sadist for millions of masochists.

A recreation for many, a profession for a few.

A sport that is very true to life with many highs and lows along the fairways of years.

The only game that has a handicap system that enables all ages and both genders to compete against one another as equals.

The above are some of the true facts relating to a game we all love.

There have also been many comical situations and many that could break your heart but those who survive show true character and would probably have done so in any other walk of life.

I have always maintained that you could tell the basic character of a person by playing a round of golf with him or her. For your character will come to the fore. The game that we have adopted which has become a religion for many, ruined marriages, businesses and friendships has also done the opposite many times and I feel that this is why we are addicted, for we have no idea what's around the next dog-leg.

This book of golf quotations will help you relax after a bad round and make you more relaxed after a good one – has to be a must for any discerning golfer to add to his or her library.

Instead of counting birdies when trying to get to sleep at night read a few quotations and dream about the best round of your life.

Yours aye,
Brian Barnes

BIBLIOGRAPHY

BOOKS

Alliss, Peter	"An Autobiography" (with Bob Ferrier)
	"Lasting the Course" (London, 1984)
	"The Open" (with Michael Hobbs, 1984)
Bamberger, Michael	"To the Linksland" (New York, 1990)
Cannon, David	"Severiano Ballesteros" (London, 1986)
Carter, John	"Play the Masters" (London, 1992)
Chieger, Bob & O'Sullivan, Pat	"Inside Golf" (New York, 1985)
Delery, John	"The Golfer's Companion" (New York, 1992)
Doust, Dudley	"Seve – the Young Champion" (London, 1982)
Fine, Alan	"Mind Over Golf" (London, 1993)
Gallwey, Timothy	"The Inner Game of Golf" (London, 1979)
Gibson, William	"Early Irish Golf" (Kildare, 1988)
Glynn, Enda	"A Century of Golf at Lahinch"
Graham, David	"Mental Toughness Training for Golf" (London, 1990)
	"Guinness Guide to Golf Equipment" (London, 1993)
Grout, Jack	"Let me Teach you Golf as I Taught Jack Nicklaus" (London, 1977)
Hope, Bob	"Confessions of a Hooker" (New York, 1993)
Hopkins, John	"The Four Majors" (London, 1988)
	"Nick Faldo in Perspective" (1986)
Jacobsen, Peter	"Buried Lies" (New York, 1993)
Jarvie, Gordon	"Great Golf Stories" (London, 1993)
Jones, Robert & Keeler, OB	"Down the Fairway" (London, 1990)
Jones, Robert	"Golf is My Game" (London, 1960)
Jones, Robert Trent	"Great Golf Stories" (New York, 1992)
Leadbetter, David	"The Golf Swing" (London, 1990)
Lucas, "Laddie"	"The Sport of Princes"
	"John Jacobs' Impact on Golf"
Michelmore, Cliff	"The Businessman's Book of Golf"
Mulqueen, Charlie	"Ireland's Top Golf Courses" (Kerry, 1990)
Murphy, Michael	"Golf in the Kingdom" (New York, 1992)

Neary, Michael	"The Golf Quiz Book" (Dublin, 1994)
O'Connor, Christy Jr	"Golf Masterclass" (London, 1993)
O'Connor, Tom	"From the Wood to the Tees" (London, 1992)
Palmer, Arnold	"My Game and Yours" (London, 1969)
Penick, Harvey	"The Little Red Golf Book" (New York, 1993)
Player, Gary	"To Be the Best" (London, 1991)
Plimpton, George	"The Bogey Man" (New York, 1968)
Redmond, John	"Great Golf Courses of Ireland" (Dublin, 1992)
Smith, Peter & Mackie, Keith	"The Guinness Book of Golf" (London, 1992)
Smith, Seamus (Ed.)	"Himself: Christy O'Connor"
Stanley, Louis	"A History of Golf"
Tibballs, Geoff	"Great Sporting Failures" (London, 1993)
Trevino, Lee	"Super Mex: an Autobiography"
Wodehouse, PG	"The Golf Omnibus" (London, 1973)

MAGAZINES

Fairways
Fore
Today's Golfer
Golf Digest
Golf Monthly
Golf World
Golfer's Companion

NEWSPAPERS

Evening Herald
Evening Press
Irish Independent
Irish Press
Irish Times
The Guardian
The Observer
The Times
The Sunday Independent
The Sunday Press
The Sunday Times
The Sunday Tribune
The Sunday World